WRITINGS OF A
CAVE MAN

THE PSALMS OF DAVID
KING OF ISRAEL

BY

JIM KING

CAVE MAN: THE PSALMS OF DAVID, KING OF ISRAEL
©2009 JIM KING MINISTRIES

International Standard Book Number: 978-0-9816884-7-3
Scripture quotations taken from:
New King James Version
The Message by Eugene Peterson

Design by Jones House Creative
www.joneshousecreative.com
Cover Photo: *Pictorial Library of Bible Lands*
www.bibleplaces.org

FOR INFORMATION:
Jim King Ministries
P.O. Box 700221
Tulsa, OK 74170

www.jimking.org

TABLE OF CONTENTS

FOREWORD

1.	Whom Are You Kissing?	9
2.	Mushrooms Everywhere	13
3.	Sleep Like a Baby	17
4.	Enjoy the Dance	21
5.	God Is Not Mad at You	25
6.	Boomerang	30
7.	Tiny Is Big	33
8.	"W"	38
9.	Pass the Test	41
10.	Thunder	45
11.	I Can See Clearly Now	49
12.	Fools Talk	53
13.	I Want to Live in a Big House	57
14.	Right Hand Benefits	61
15.	Apple of Your Eye	66
16.	Humpty Dumpty	69
17.	The Secret Is Out	73
18.	He Took Off Their Chariot Wheels	77
19.	No Sweat	81
20.	Sing, Momma, Sing	87
21.	Bloodhounds	91
22.	James Bond Stuff	95
23.	Stuck in the Middle	100
24.	Integrity	103
25.	You Can't Eat Me	108
26.	Heart Break Ridge	111
27.	Tah-Wa-He	115
28.	Joy Is Around the Corner	119
29.	The Last Words of Jesus	124
30.	Mules	127
31.	Change Your Act	132
32.	The Invisible Man	135
33.	No Comparison	139
34.	Economic Injustice	143

35.	Ouch!	148
36.	Big Troublemaker	151
37.	Dead Sea Mud	156
38.	Opportunity Is Everywhere	159
39.	Get Real, Man!	164
40.	Facebook	167
41.	Fear? What Fear?	171
42.	Wrong Side of the Mountain	175
43.	Backstabber	180
44.	Unfortunately, It's an Old Soviet Airplane	183
45.	Cave Man	187
46.	Deaf Cobra	191
47.	Eye of the Storm	196
48.	God's Will Is God's Bill	199
49.	Under the Big Tent	203
50.	Talk to Yourself	207
51.	Keep the Motor Running	211
52.	Cat and Mouse Game	215
53.	Awesome Cheeseburger	219
54.	Pure Religion	223
55.	Squeaky Wheel Gets the Grease	227
56.	Confused	231
57.	Ready, Set, Go	236
58.	The Key to Everything	239
59.	Be a Good Boy	243
60.	Tie a String Around Your Finger	248
61.	In the Zone	251
62.	Skin and Bones	256
63.	I'm Not Kenny G	259
64.	"P"	263
65.	Your Side of the Ball	267
66.	Out of My League	271
67.	God Says, "Wow!"	275
68.	Boats and Gods	279
69.	He Does Not Think Like Me	284
70.	Snake Poison	287
71.	Ivory Soap	291
72.	Cave Visitors	295
73.	Good Teachers	300
74.	Great Kids	304
75.	Gravy Over All	308

FOREWORD

David, the shepherd boy who became the king of Israel, has long been one of my favorite characters in the Bible. God Himself said in His Word, "I have found David the son of Jesse, a man after My own heart, who will do all My will" (Acts 13:22 NKJV). David was a man who enjoyed a deep, intimate relationship with the God he loved, yet he also knew the bitter pain of failing Him miserably. David was a man we all can relate to on some level. Perhaps that is why God imparted to him many of the psalms. Three thousand years after they were written, these psalms are still being read, quoted, preached, and sung around the world.

David faced many battles in his life. Like him, our course in life is largely determined by how we handle both victories and setbacks. We can learn from his example and writings.

If you read David's writings closely, you will realize he confronted issues that many people face today. He apparently lacked his father's full vote of approval. He had sibling dynamics, being one of eight brothers. He endured loss of loved ones, betrayal by friends and colleagues, and even betrayal and rebellion from his own son. He perhaps lacked the greatest of parenting skills. David conquered many foes on the battlefield, yet utterly failed when tempted with sin in his flesh. He committed the very two sins for which the Law required a death sentence – murder and adultery. The good news is he found refuge in the arms of a loving God Who unequivocally forgives all sin.

David knew the power of a truly repentant heart and the even greater power of an unconditionally loving God. I pray that, in reading his psalms, you too will realize just how much God does really love you. He cares about the outcome of every test and challenge you may face today. God is for you as much as He was for David.

This book is in no way an exhaustive effort to understand all that David wrote in his psalms, nor is it an examination of all the psalms in the Bible. Most Bible historians believe David authored 75 of the 150 psalms in the Book of Psalms. For our purposes, we will be focusing only on the 75 Psalms of David. Because David was such a worshipper, I am convinced he authored other psalms as well.

Please let me tell you my reason for writing before you begin your devotional journey with King David. One morning in my devotions, during a challenging season in my life, I felt the voice of the Lord whisper to me clearly, "Meditate the Psalms of David." It was very distinct. God did not say the Psalms, but the Psalms of David. To meditate on these psalms would mean "to dwell on them a little while; to chew over in my spirit and mind what David said."

So I began to do this in my devotions as the Lord instructed. I began to see things David had written in a brighter light. I took time to not only think about what was being said, but I also opened the door for the Lord to speak to me about what I was reading. I took one Psalm of David per day, allowing it to speak to me. I experienced conviction about things I did not even realize were wrong (see devotion of Psalm 19). I also experienced great encouragement in my faith, determination to press on through challenges, and a deeper desire to draw closer to this ever-amazing God David wrote so much about. I hope you experience the same.

Perhaps you thought the book title a bit unusual. That was intentional. The first image most people have of David is either as shepherd, king, or giant killer. Instead of examining David as shepherd or king, I chose to focus on the image of cave man. David spent considerable time in caves, hiding from his pursuers. The cover picture is a cave. From the caves were penned some of the psalms we enjoy. These life experiences and David's response to them are what transformed him into a king.

I have intentionally titled many of the devotions with an unusual title. My intent is to give you something catchy and easy to remember throughout the day after you have had your devotions. I have done this myself while writing the book. It is good to meditate on God's Word throughout the day. These little titles help me to easily remember what I studied that morning. My writings are intentionally brief on each psalm because my intent is for the book to be a devotional. Most people live very busy lives. What I have written from each psalm can be read in a few minutes. All Scripture references are from the New King James Version unless otherwise noted.

Perhaps, you will want to read the entire psalm as well as the devotional commentary. If you do, I know God will speak much more to your heart than I could ever imagine. I have included extra pages throughout the book to make it convenient for you to journal your thoughts. I also know there are many people who can write more brilliantly than me about David's Psalms. Thank you for letting me share a brief glimpse into some of the things God has emphasized to me as I have meditated the Psalms of David.

Only by making room for God in our lives every day can we begin to realize the magnitude of His deep love for us. I am convinced that David, King of Israel, found such a love. For David, life was a journey of getting to know his God on a deeper level day by day. I pray you experience the same love as you daily walk with Him. As you grow in your desire to follow God, you will be able to say as David, "I delight to do your will, O my God" (Psalm 40:8). Therein lies the key to success in the eyes of God.

Enjoy the journey,
Jim King

PSALM 2
NEW KING JAMES VERSION

1 "Why do the nations rage,
And the people plot a vain thing?
2 The kings of the earth set themselves,
And the rulers take counsel together,
Against the LORD and against His Anointed, saying,
3 'Let us break Their bonds in pieces
And cast away Their cords from us.'

4 He who sits in the heavens shall laugh;
The Lord shall hold them in derision.
5 Then He shall speak to them in His wrath,
And distress them in His deep displeasure:
6 'Yet I have set My King
On My holy hill of Zion.'

7 I will declare the decree:
The LORD has said to Me,
'You are My Son,
Today I have begotten You.
8 Ask of Me, and I will give You
The nations for Your inheritance,
And the ends of the earth for Your possession.
9 You shall break them with a rod of iron;
You shall dash them to pieces like a potter's vessel.'

10 Now therefore, be wise, O kings;
Be instructed, you judges of the earth.
11 Serve the LORD with fear,
And rejoice with trembling.
12 Kiss the Son, lest He be angry,
And you perish in the way,
When His wrath is kindled but a little.
Blessed are all those who put their trust in Him."

1
WHOM ARE YOU KISSING?
PSALM 2

To our western mindset, a kiss is a symbol of affection between family, close friends, or lovers. But in eastern cultures, a kiss has a significantly different connotation. The dictionary defines to kiss as "to touch or press with the lips slightly pursed in token of greeting, affection, or reverence." The three words "greeting, affection and reverence" shed some light on the phrase "kiss the Son" mentioned in Psalm 2:12. This psalm, which focuses on the Messiah and His kingdom, is a call for reverence and submission to the King.

Since this psalm was written about 3,000 years ago, we must understand the eastern culture's purpose for a kiss to grasp its meaning. The Hebrew word for "kiss" in this verse is *nashak*, which means "submit to or be ruled by." The word occurs thirty-two times in the Old Testament. As I began to look at other places in Scripture where this same word appears, I gained a greater understanding of "kiss" and its applications in the Bible. Let's look at three instances where the term "kiss" is used.

In Genesis 27, Isaac, the son of Abraham, was about to die. He called in his son, Jacob, whose name God later changed to Israel, to pronounce a final blessing upon him. Isaac said, "Come near now and kiss me, my son. And he came near and kissed him" (verse 27). From here, Isaac proceeded to pronounce blessing on Jacob. This generational blessing contained three aspects: material prosperity (verse 28), political supremacy (verse 29), and a cursing of all enemies (verse 29). Jacob kissed Isaac, a sign to Isaac of submission.

Nashak also appears in I Samuel 10:1: "Then Samuel took a flask of oil and poured it on his (Saul's) head, and kissed him…" At this point Israel had never had a king. This was new territory, yet Samuel, God's prophet, recognized his need to submit to the authority of this God-appointed king.

Finally, *nashak* appears in I Kings 19. Elijah the prophet had just killed 850 false prophets of Baal who were sponsored by the wicked rulers, Ahab and Jezebel. Jezebel threatened to kill Elijah, who ran into the wilderness wanting to die. Feeling alone in his worship of the one true God, Elijah was absorbed in self-pity. God quickly interrupted his pity-party when He told Elijah: "I have reserved seven thousand in Israel, all whose knees have not bowed to Baal, and every mouth that has not kissed him" (verse 18). Elijah thought everyone had kissed (submitted to) Baal, and only he had kissed (submitted to) God. Maybe he should have asked others the question "Whom are you kissing?" Perhaps their answer would have encouraged him!

Although I cannot speak for anyone else, I fully intend to "kiss the Son." I encourage you to join me in this act of submission to our Lord and King. With David's words echoing in our hearts, may we strive to daily submit and yield to the Son. He is the only God worthy of our reverence, devotion, and submission.

NOTES:

PSALM 3
THE MESSAGE BIBLE

1-2 God! Look! Enemies past counting!
Enemies sprouting like mushrooms,
Mobs of them all around me, roaring their mockery:
"Hah! No help for him from God!"

3-4 But you, God, shield me on all sides;
You ground my feet, you lift my head high;
With all my might I shout up to God,
His answers thunder from the holy mountain.

5-6 I stretch myself out. I sleep.
Then I'm up again—rested, tall and steady,
Fearless before the enemy mobs
Coming at me from all sides.

7 Up, God! My God, help me!
Slap their faces,
First this cheek, then the other,
Your fist hard in their teeth!

8 Real help comes from God.
Your blessing clothes your people!

2

Mushrooms Everywhere
Psalm 3

Trouble everywhere! That was how David felt at this moment. He started his psalm by saying, "God! Look! Enemies past counting! Enemies sprouting like mushrooms" (MSG). Although I am not a mushroom expert, I can imagine David's enemies surrounding him like hundreds of mushrooms springing up all over the ground.

We live in Oklahoma where most lawns have Bermuda grass, as does ours. Last summer we had several wild mushrooms sprout up in our lawn. This spring Pam planted a new flower bed. Recently, I heard her say, "This bed has mushrooms everywhere!" We did nothing we knew of to make this happen; the mushrooms just appeared one day.

Our enemies (problems) tend to sprout up unexpectedly like mushrooms. Thankfully, mushrooms are easy to eliminate. (I quickly purged our yard of the mushroom invasion.) To God, your problems are easy to handle. That is why David, while surrounded by a multitude of enemies, turned immediately to the Lord. In this verse, David was basically saying: "Without God, you are in trouble; with God, your enemy is in trouble, no matter how many there are!"

When David wrote this psalm, he was experiencing something he never dreamed could happen. His own son, Absalom, was leading a rebellion against him. To make matters worse, thousands of David's former loyal subjects had joined forces with Absalom (verse 1). David was being forced to flee for his life from Jerusalem, yet he wrote this psalm in the process.

Not only was David facing all these problems sprouting around him, but his heart was also suffering immense pain. Can you imagine the heartache David was going through? First, his own flesh and blood was out to kill him. How that must have grieved his father-heart! If Absalom's hatred and rebellion weren't enough, the men who had once pledged their allegiance to David now wanted him dead as well. David must have felt like the most used, despised, and betrayed man in history. His heart was breaking to pieces as he penned this psalm.

Some of you reading this may be experiencing heartache greater than you ever imagined possible. It would be nice if being a follower of Christ exempted us from such experiences. Of course, that is not the case. Even our Lord endured heartache when all forsook Him prior to His crucifixion. He was there alone to suffer the consequences of all our sins. *But that was the last time one of God's people would ever be alone.* After Jesus rose from the dead and ascended to the Father, He made this promise: "I am with you always, even to the end of the age" (Matthew 28:20). Jesus also said, "I will pray the Father, and He will give you another helper." You have the Holy Spirit with you and in you always! (See John 14:17.)

As a Christian, you are never alone. Throughout today, know that God is with you. Take time to acknowledge His presence and talk to Him. Can you imagine spending all day with someone and never speaking to him? How awkward and useless that would be! Don't let this happen in your relationship with the Lord. Draw close to Him in prayer. First Thessalonians 5:17 admonishes us to pray without ceasing. God is on your side, and He is there to help you in every situation in life.

David talked to God about his problems. He wrote in Psalm 3:3: "But You, O Lord, are a shield for me, My glory and the One who lifts up my head." In verse 4, David said he cried to the Lord, and the Lord heard him. Verse 5 notes how David ended his day in restful sleep without fear. What more could one ask for? If you call out to God, He will "lift your head" above your pain and problems. He will give you peace and rest.

If your problems are surrounding you like mushrooms, remember

God can quickly deliver you. If you're suffering pain in your heart, take it to the heart-healer. Even with his best efforts, man cannot heal heartache. Only God can heal the brokenhearted. Today, remember these words of Jesus recorded in Luke 4:18: "The Spirit of the Lord is upon Me...He has sent Me to heal the brokenhearted, To proclaim liberty to the captives... To set at liberty those who are oppressed" (NKJV). Walk and talk with the Healer of heartaches throughout the day and sleep like a baby tonight.

PSALM 4
NEW KING JAMES VERSION

¹ Hear me when I call, O God of my righteousness!
You have relieved me in my distress;
Have mercy on me, and hear my prayer.

² How long, O you sons of men,
Will you turn my glory to shame?
How long will you love worthlessness
And seek falsehood? Selah
³ But know that the LORD has set apart
for Himself him who is godly;
The LORD will hear when I call to Him.

⁴ Be angry, and do not sin.
Meditate within your heart on your bed, and be still. Selah
⁵ Offer the sacrifices of righteousness,
And put your trust in the LORD.

⁶ There are many who say,
"Who will show us any good?"
LORD, lift up the light of Your countenance upon us.
⁷ You have put gladness in my heart,
More than in the season that their grain and wine increased.
⁸ I will both lie down in peace, and sleep;
For You alone, O LORD, make me dwell in safety.

3

SLEEP LIKE A BABY
PSALM 4

David wrote this psalm in the midst of fleeing from his son, Absalom, who was leading a rebellion against David in an attempt to take the throne. In verse 7, David credited God for putting gladness in his heart more than in the time when "corn and wine increased." This phrase is always expressive of temporal blessings. In other words, David was saying he had more joy in the hard places of life than in times when everything appeared to be going good. On the surface, David's circumstances looked disastrous; but things are not always as they appear. In one of the darkest hours of his life, David found joy in God. How do you find joy and peace in a time like that?

You may find a key as you lie in bed at night in those moments before you go to sleep. Two of the eight verses in Psalm 4 (verses 4 and 8) instruct us to meditate during these dark and quiet moments. As you drift off into slumber, remember all of the times God has been faithful to you, just as David meditated on the past faithfulness of God (verse 1).

The King James Version of verse 8 says: "I will both lay me down in peace and sleep." Notice the word "both." God wants you to sleep like a baby, but you have to lie down. You can't sleep in peace while pacing the floor in worry. When the pressures of life begin to overwhelm you, do not give in by staying up and worrying. Take the faith step of lying down with the intent of sleeping in peace. Meditate on God's Word and His past faithfulness to you and sleep like a baby.

David knew only God could provide real peace. Peace is a major indicator of the presence of God. Satan is the antithesis of peace. He brings turmoil, fear, worry, and insecurity. Colossians 3:15 tells us that the "peace of God" is to "rule our hearts." The Greek word for "rule" in this verse means "umpire." God's peace is to literally be the umpire of our lives.

An umpire is in charge of the whole game. What he says goes, even when it may not seem right. Although earthly umpires may miss it sometimes, God never does. Let Him call the shots in your life. He is always right.

Learn to trust this inner guidance system of God's peace. As you do, you will be like David who said God's peace allowed him to "lie down and sleep" and made him "dwell in safety and confident trust." What a wonderful way to live! God wants you to enjoy life worry-free. He is faithful to take care of any situation facing you.

Jesus said in Matthew 6:31-33: "Do not worry, saying, 'What shall we eat?' or 'What shall we drink?' or 'What shall we wear?'... Your heavenly Father knows that you need all these things. But seek first the kingdom of God and His righteousness, and all these things shall be added to you." Since our Heavenly Father promises to take care of us, we can trust Him, relax, and sleep like a baby!

NOTES:

PSALM 5
NEW KING JAMES VERSION

1 Give ear to my words, O LORD,
Consider my meditation.
2 Give heed to the voice of my cry,
My King and my God, for to You I will pray.
3 My voice You shall hear in the morning, O LORD;
In the morning I will direct it to You,
And I will look up.
4 For You are not a God who takes pleasure in wickedness,
Nor shall evil dwell with You.
5 The boastful shall not stand in Your sight;
You hate all workers of iniquity.
6 You shall destroy those who speak falsehood;
The LORD abhors the bloodthirsty and deceitful man.
7 But as for me, I will come into Your house
in the multitude of Your mercy;
In fear of You I will worship toward Your holy temple.
8 Lead me, O LORD, in Your righteousness
because of my enemies;
Make Your way straight before my face.
9 For there is no faithfulness in their mouth;
Their inward part is destruction;
Their throat is an open tomb;
They flatter with their tongue.
10 Pronounce them guilty, O God!
Let them fall by their own counsels;
Cast them out in the multitude of their transgressions,
For they have rebelled against You.
11 But let all those rejoice who put their trust in You;
Let them ever shout for joy, because You defend them;
Let those also who love Your name be joyful in You.
12 For You, O LORD, will bless the righteous;
With favor You will surround him as with a shield.

4

Enjoy the Dance
Psalm 5

I am not a dancer, probably because I would crush my wife's toes if I tried. I have had no lessons or training in dance. I am told that when an experienced dancer is joined with an inexperienced dancer, he will say, "Just relax and follow my lead." When it comes to following God, life is like a dance. We relax and follow His lead. When we need guidance in our daily affairs, important decisions, or matters of the heart, we can just follow the Leader and trust Him to guide us in the right way.

At many points in his life, David was in need of guidance from the Lord. Psalm 5 is one specific prayer for guidance. David made it very clear he desired God to lead him (verses 2, 3, 7, 8). Can you imagine the magnitude of decisions that came David's way? The responsibility he felt was extreme. Like David, we all have responsibilities. We may not be rulers of an entire nation, but our lives are filled with responsibility.

Humans are prone to errors both in judgment and choices. David recognized that only God has perfect judgment and never errs in His choices. Can you trust the choices He has made for you? Psalm 5:11 says, "Let all those rejoice who put their trust in You." Trust is easy when things are going like we think they should. It is more difficult when life's road turns a direction we weren't planning.

Maybe today you're at a point in life where the road has taken you in a different direction than you were planning. Some of you might have lost a job, a friend, or a loved one. Perhaps others have lost someone you leaned heavily upon. When these unexpected events occur in life, we are confronted with the responsibility of making decisions. Perhaps they are decisions we are not comfortable making, but they must be made nevertheless.

Psalm 5:8 says that it is God who must lead us. Set your heart to follow Him and Him alone. He never makes a bad choice. I love the words of Jesus in John 10:27, 28 (AMP): "The sheep that are My own hear and are listening to My voice; and I know them and they follow Me. And I give them eternal life, and they shall never lose it or perish throughout the ages. [To all eternity they shall never by any means be destroyed.] And no one is able to snatch them out of My hand." What a promise! The sheep that are listening to the voice of God and following Him shall never be destroyed!

As a sheep following the Good Shepherd, you can live free from fear. Fear paralyzes. Do not let fear intimidate you. Declare that you will make the right choices today and every day because God is leading you. Many blessings in life have been missed because someone was fearful or uncertain and consequently did nothing. God has called us to lives of productivity and prosperity as we follow Him. Only He gives the ability to be a success. Be sure He has your next success planned in life as you follow His lead.

Whenever you need guidance, remember to let Jesus lead you in the dance. Listen carefully for His voice and keep in step with Him. Sit back, relax, and enjoy the dance!

NOTES:

PSALM 6
NEW KING JAMES VERSION

---

1 O LORD, do not rebuke me in Your anger,
Nor chasten me in Your hot displeasure.
2 Have mercy on me, O LORD, for I am weak;
O LORD, heal me, for my bones are troubled.
3 My soul also is greatly troubled;
But You, O LORD—how long?

4 Return, O LORD, deliver me!
Oh, save me for Your mercies' sake!
5 For in death there is no remembrance of You;
In the grave who will give You thanks?

6 I am weary with my groaning;
All night I make my bed swim;
I drench my couch with my tears.
7 My eye wastes away because of grief;
It grows old because of all my enemies.

8 Depart from me, all you workers of iniquity;
For the LORD has heard the voice of my weeping.
9 The LORD has heard my supplication;
The LORD will receive my prayer.
10 Let all my enemies be ashamed and greatly troubled;
Let them turn back and be ashamed suddenly.

5

GOD IS NOT MAD AT YOU
PSALM 6

Have you ever felt like God was mad at you? If you've ever felt that way, it's important for you to realize this one truth: God is never mad at you. Don't misunderstand, God does get angry. Psalm 6:1 makes that very clear. He gets mad at sin and its source.

Being made in God's image insures we will experience the emotion of anger. Anger is a God-given emotion. Therefore we are admonished in Ephesians 4:26: "Be angry, and do not sin." God has never sinned by punishing in anger. In fact, Scripture teaches the exact opposite, that He chastens those He loves. Proverbs 3:12 says, "Whom the Lord loves, He corrects, just as a father the son in whom he delights." Hebrews 12:5,6 says, "Do not...be discouraged when you are rebuked by Him; for whom the Lord loves he chastens."

Sadly, there have been many earthly parents who have struck their children in anger. One of the saddest days of my life was when our son, Drew, was a small boy. He had misbehaved and angered me. I gave him a spanking while I was angry. Although that incident happened about twenty years ago, it still brings tears to my eyes as I am writing this. I was wrong! God convicted me strongly. Soon I found myself kneeling before my young son and asking his forgiveness. I told him his actions did deserve discipline but I was completely wrong in the way I had administered it. We prayed together, and although I felt slightly better, I have never forgotten it to this day. I know my son did not deserve that.

Now, can you imagine God kneeling before you and saying, "I was wrong, forgive Me?" No way! He is without sin. You see, God would never punish you in anger. He never manifests evil to produce good. Never believe the lie that God is mad at you and that is why you are suffering with an illness or experiencing a particular problem. He is a good God. James 1:16,17 says, "Do not be deceived, my beloved brethren. Every good and perfect gift is from above, coming down from the Father..." Good things come from God. Satan wants you deceived into believing that bad things happen because God is mad at you. Never believe that lie because it is not true. God is not mad at you!

In Psalm 6, David asked God for mercy. It seems David was afraid God was mad at him, and he made excuses for himself before God in verse 2. Coming tenderly before the Lord is a good idea, and God is faithful to extend His mercy. But God is not short-tempered like man. He would never destroy or harm you in anger like another human can be tempted to do. Do not assign human characteristics to your idea of God. Rather, focus on continually developing godlike characteristics in your life. After the experience with my son, I determined with God's help to not do anything like that again. Ask God to give you a clear understanding of His ways. Unlike ours, God's ways are completely pure, holy, and righteous.

Sometimes, we do have to process what is going on in our lives. Perhaps that is what David was doing in Psalm 6. He was processing the feelings of insecurity in his relationship with God in verses 1 through 3. In verses 4 and 5, he came to his senses and cried out to God for help; in verses 6 and 7, he described his feelings to God.

In the last part of the psalm, faith and hope began to arise in David's heart. He declared, "Because the Lord has heard my prayer, the enemy had better leave!" That place of faith and hope is where God wants you and me to live. We're not to dwell in the realm of doubt and fear, thinking God is mad at us or punishing us. We are to live in the realm where faith and hope abound. God is for you! Today, declare as the

Apostle Paul did in Romans 8:31: "If God is for us, who can be against us?"

PSALM 7
NEW KING JAMES VERSION

¹ O LORD my God, in You I put my trust;
Save me from all those who persecute me;
And deliver me,
² Lest they tear me like a lion,
Rending me in pieces, while there is none to deliver.

³ O LORD my God, if I have done this:
If there is iniquity in my hands,
⁴ If I have repaid evil to him who was at peace with me,
Or have plundered my enemy without cause,
⁵ Let the enemy pursue me and overtake me;
Yes, let him trample my life to the earth,
And lay my honor in the dust. Selah

⁶ Arise, O LORD, in Your anger;
Lift Yourself up because of the rage of my enemies;
Rise up for me to the judgment You have commanded!
⁷ So the congregation of the peoples shall surround You;
For their sakes, therefore, return on high.
⁸ The LORD shall judge the peoples;
Judge me, O LORD, according to my righteousness,
And according to my integrity within me.

⁹ Oh, let the wickedness of the wicked come to an end,
But establish the just;
For the righteous God tests the hearts and minds.
¹⁰ My defense is of God,
Who saves the upright in heart.

¹¹ God is a just judge,
And God is angry with the wicked every day.
¹² If he does not turn back,
He will sharpen His sword;
He bends His bow and makes it ready.

¹³ He also prepares for Himself instruments of death;
He makes His arrows into fiery shafts.

¹⁴ Behold, the wicked brings forth iniquity;
Yes, he conceives trouble and brings forth falsehood.
¹⁵ He made a pit and dug it out,
And has fallen into the ditch which he made.
¹⁶ His trouble shall return upon his own head,
And his violent dealing shall come down on his own crown.

¹⁷ I will praise the LORD according to His righteousness,
And will sing praise to the name of the LORD Most High.

6
BOOMERANG
PSALM 7

Psalm 7 was written during a negative experience David had with "Cush, a Benjamite." Cush is referred to in Scripture only here. Who he was remains unknown, but he was probably a relative of King Saul. From this passage, it appears David had been slandered. In praying for deliverance from his slanderous enemies, David affirmed his innocence while appealing to God for vindication.

Scripture records David being the recipient of such injustice on more than one occasion. Most Bible scholars believe David wrote this psalm when he was fleeing from Saul's men. Saul had unjustly tried to kill David twenty-one times, but God continued to deliver him. Saul had also falsely accused David of trying to assassinate him and take over his kingdom. If you are keeping score, the score is against David. He is outnumbered and being slandered.

If you have experienced unjust accusation, you know it doesn't feel good. No matter how unjust the circumstances, it's important for you to not retaliate out of your feelings. Reacting from your feelings won't do any good anyway. Instead, follow David's example and go to God in times of persecution. In Psalm 7:1, 2, David released his vindication to God. He indicated that if God did not come to his rescue, he would be destroyed like a lion rending his prey into pieces.

Have you ever sat in a courtroom? Two sides tell their story and a judge decides who is right. Through much of David's life, the "other side" told wild, untrue stories about him. Perhaps some of you have experienced something like that. Maybe you have experienced an unjust lawsuit. Perhaps you have a neighbor who simply does not like you and makes up stories about you to other neighbors. That may sound silly, but it happens. You may be experiencing jealousy on the other person's part. Saul obviously was jealous of David.

In a courtroom, any good judge can detect a crazy story a mile away. You have the Judge of the entire universe on your side. This psalm reveals Him as a just Judge who will judge us according to our righteousness. Focus on doing what is right, not on what someone else is doing wrong. God will take care of it. Verses 15 and 16 reveal that the wicked fall into their own trap. Their wickedness will boomerang on them.

Satan is the ultimate false accuser. We know what is awaiting him. If you have repented of your sins, do not allow the false accuser to whisper condemnation in your ear. He is a liar and the just Judge in heaven knows you are clean in His eyes. Revelation 12:10 says: "Now salvation, and strength, and the kingdom of our God, and the power of His Christ has come, for the accuser of our brethren (Satan), who accused them before our God day and night, has been cast down."

The just Judge of the universe has thrown every false accusation against you out of His courtroom. So whenever you are faced with false accusations or persecution, turn it over to the Lord. He will vindicate you.

PSALM 8
NEW KING JAMES VERSION

¹ O LORD, our Lord,
How excellent is Your name in all the earth,
Who have set Your glory above the heavens!

² Out of the mouth of babes and nursing infants
You have ordained strength,
Because of Your enemies,
That You may silence the enemy and the avenger.

³ When I consider Your heavens, the work of Your fingers,
The moon and the stars, which You have ordained,
4 What is man that You are mindful of him,
And the son of man that You visit him?
⁵ For You have made him a little lower than the angels,
And You have crowned him with glory and honor.

⁶ You have made him to have dominion over the works of Your hands;
You have put all things under his feet,
⁷ All sheep and oxen—
Even the beasts of the field,
⁸ The birds of the air,
And the fish of the sea
That pass through the paths of the seas.

⁹ O LORD, our Lord,
How excellent is Your name in all the earth!

7
TINY IS BIG
PSALM 8

Everyone has moments in life when it seems like God is distant. But according to Psalm 8, God is not distant from humanity. In those moments when it seems God is far away, do what David did. He decided to look around and see that God is everywhere. In verse 3 he said, "When I consider Your heavens, the work of Your fingers..." It is hard to be encouraged if you do not take time to "consider" (think about it). Clearly, David was not dwelling on his feelings, but making a conscious decision to see God in every circumstance and place.

This kind of contemplation reveals how small we are and how big God is. He is so big that the authors in the Bible couldn't even describe Him. Isaiah made an attempt in Isaiah 40:12. He declared, "He has measured the waters (of the world) in the hollow of his hand." Now that is big! Last week Pam and I were on the shore of the Pacific Ocean near San Diego. I looked at the vast ocean in front of me and quoted this verse. It was vast, but I was only looking at a drop in a bucket. Imagine how much water there is on this earth. Your God held it all, not just a part of one ocean, in the hollow of His hand. He is certainly big enough to handle the mountain in front of you today.

I remember as a small boy we had a family friend with monstrous hands. Everyone called him "Tiny." There was nothing tiny about him, especially his hands. When he shook hands with someone, his hand would swallow the other person's. No one wanted to mess with him because of his intimidating size.

That's how your enemy, Satan, needs to feel. Satan doesn't want to mess with God because He knows how big He is. He remembers how God threw him out of Heaven long ago. (See Isaiah 14:12-15; Luke 10:18.) Satan only wants to mess with you! Inform him today that you are calling on God to be your defender and protector. David started this psalm with, "O Lord, our Lord, how excellent (majestic and glorious) is Your name in all the earth" (AMP). Declare His name. Your enemy knows well Who you are talking about.

Isaiah went on to say, "He measured the heavens with a span." The Amplified Bible says a "span" is nine inches, which is the average size of the span of a man's hand. Tiny's hand seemed twice that to me. Sometimes, tiny is actually big! Go outside and look at the sky. Again, you are only looking at the proverbial "drop in a bucket." The heavens extend on forever. How many galaxies exist that are not yet discovered by man? The answer is unknown. The God of the universe is definitely big enough to handle the mountain in front of you. He already proved He is big enough to handle Satan very easily. Whatever problem you are facing, simply turn it over to Him.

All we need to know today is that God is bigger than any problem. To you, your problem may appear gigantic, but to God, it is but a speck of dust. Trust Him. He has given you "dominion" (Psalm 8:6). Dominion means "the power or right of governing or controlling." In His goodness, God gave man dominion in the earth. Based on these words, I do not believe God wants your life to be an out-of-control life. There is nothing outside the power of God's control. He has given us the "right" to have dominion, not because of who we are, but because "Greater is He Who is in you than he who is in the world" (I John 4:4). He is big enough.

NOTES:

PSALM 9
NEW KING JAMES VERSION

1 I will praise You, O LORD, with my whole heart;
I will tell of all Your marvelous works.
2 I will be glad and rejoice in You;
I will sing praise to Your name, O Most High.

3 When my enemies turn back,
They shall fall and perish at Your presence.
4 For You have maintained my right and my cause;
You sat on the throne judging in righteousness.
5 You have rebuked the nations,
You have destroyed the wicked;
You have blotted out their name forever and ever.

6 O enemy, destructions are finished forever!
And you have destroyed cities;
Even their memory has perished.
7 But the LORD shall endure forever;
He has prepared His throne for judgment.
8 He shall judge the world in righteousness,
And He shall administer judgment for the peoples in uprightness.

9 The LORD also will be a refuge for the oppressed,
A refuge in times of trouble.
10 And those who know Your name will put their trust in You;
For You, LORD, have not forsaken those who seek You.
11 Sing praises to the LORD, who dwells in Zion!
Declare His deeds among the people.
12 When He avenges blood, He remembers them;
He does not forget the cry of the humble.

13 Have mercy on me, O LORD!
Consider my trouble from those who hate me,
You who lift me up from the gates of death,

¹⁴ That I may tell of all Your praise
In the gates of the daughter of Zion.
I will rejoice in Your salvation.

¹⁵ The nations have sunk down in the pit which they made;
In the net which they hid, their own foot is caught.
¹⁶ The LORD is known by the judgment He executes;
The wicked is snared in the work of his own hands. Selah

¹⁷ The wicked shall be turned into hell,
And all the nations that forget God.
¹⁸ For the needy shall not always be forgotten;
The expectation of the poor shall not perish forever.

¹⁹ Arise, O LORD, do not let man prevail;
Let the nations be judged in Your sight.
²⁰ Put them in fear, O LORD,
That the nations may know themselves to be but men. Selah

8

"W"
PSALM 9

The 43rd President of the United States was George W. Bush. President Bush became known to some as "W" partly because his father, the 41st President, was also George Bush. Aside from presidential nicknames, "W" can also help us remember three key points in Psalm 9 — worship, witness, and will.

Worship – Many words can be used to describe David, King of Israel. One of the most accurate is "worshipper." He was a worshipper long before he became a king. It is easy to worship when all is well. True worshippers do so at all times, no matter the temporal circumstance. David said in Psalm 34:1: "I will bless the Lord at all times; His praise shall continually be in my mouth." Regardless of what happens today, determine now to be a continual worshipper.

There is a popular chorus called "I Am a Friend of God" being sung in some churches today. The song is based on James 2:23 which tells us that Abraham was called "the friend of God." For us to have the privilege of being a friend of God, we should strive to live as Abraham did. Let's not be God's "fair weather friend," showing up just when the weather is beautiful. The Bible says that a friend loves at all times (Proverbs 17:17). A true worshipper worships at all times.

Witness – David said, "I will tell of all Your marvelous works" (verse 1). Why not tell someone today about our marvelous Lord? Although this thought may intimidate some people, don't let it intimidate you. If you remain open to the Lord, He will open little opportunities in the course of your day to tell others about Him.

One day, years ago, I was working alone at home when a magazine salesman rang the doorbell. To be honest, I was annoyed at first. I was very busy. I knew I wasn't going to buy any magazines, and his presentation would take a few of my precious minutes. However, he was so smooth I decided to listen. As he came to the end of his presentation, he made a big mistake. He said, "Mr. King, let me ask you one more question. What do you think is the single most important decision a human being can make?" For a Christian, there is only one answer to that question – to make Jesus Christ the Lord of your life. To witness to this salesman, I did not need to have a message or 200 Scriptures memorized. Witnessing only required me to tell the truth. So I answered his question. Of course, it blew his sales pitch but created a platform to witness.

Will – David said, "I will praise You, O Lord, with my whole heart" (verse 1). In the next verse he said, "I will be glad and rejoice in You." Set your will to praise God in everything, with your whole heart, and to do it with gladness. It will make for a great day.

As you go through your day today, remember these three "W's" from David. Be a worshipper, be a witness, and determine in your heart that you will praise God in everything!

PSALM 11
THE MESSAGE BIBLE

1-3 I've already run for dear life straight to the arms of God.
So why would I run away now
when you say,
"Run to the mountains; the evil
bows are bent, the wicked arrows
Aimed to shoot under cover of darkness
at every heart open to God.
The bottom's dropped out of the country;
good people don't have a chance"?

4-6 But God hasn't moved to the mountains;
his holy address hasn't changed.
He's in charge, as always, his eyes
taking everything in, his eyelids
Unblinking, examining Adam's unruly brood
inside and out, not missing a thing.
He tests the good and the bad alike;
if anyone cheats, God's outraged.
Fail the test and you're out,
out in a hail of firestones,
Drinking from a canteen
filled with hot desert wind.

7 God's business is putting things right;
he loves getting the lines straight,
Setting us straight. Once we're standing tall,
we can look him straight in the eye

9
PASS THE TEST
PSALM 11

When you see the word "test" in the Bible, do not confuse it with the word "tempt." God never tempts people with sin. James 1:13 says, "Let no man say when he is tempted, 'I am tempted by God'; for God cannot be tempted by evil, nor does He Himself tempt anyone." In Psalm 11:5 David said, "The Lord tests the righteous." When God gives a test, I want to pass the test.

You may be wondering, "How do I pass God's tests?" Like passing tests in school, you try to pass the tests in life. You put forth effort by studying and preparing yourself. That is one reason why it is important to spend time with God and in His Word every day. His Word prepares you for the tests that will come.

When a righteous person sees wicked men committing injustice, his faith and patience are tested. The Lord seems to wait momentarily to see who will remain loyal to Him. No matter what happens in the earth, I want to be in the group that remains loyal to the Lord. Testing in the Bible carries with it the idea of proving the genuineness of a person's heart.

The Message Bible is explicit here in Psalm 11. It says, "He (God) tests the good and the bad alike; if anyone cheats, God's outraged. Fail the test and you're out, out in a hail of firestones, drinking from a canteen filled with hot desert wind." Suffice it to say we want to pass God's tests.

Let's consider the purpose of a test. The greatest function of a test is for both the teacher and student to know where the student stands in relation to the subject being taught. In school, students compare themselves with each other. That is how a testing curve is established. God does not work off the curve. He does not compare us to each other, nor are we to compare ourselves with others. According to 2 Corinthians 10:12, those who compare themselves with others are not wise.

The real purpose of a test is to know where we stand in relation to where the teacher (tester) wants us to be. The teacher gives the final grade, and that is all that matters. By testing, the teacher learns if we are grasping the lessons being taught.

Do not fall into the trap of comparing yourself with others. Focus on the real purpose of testing – knowing how you are doing in your walk with God. If you see an area where your "test scores" are a little low, work on that area. Ask the Holy Spirit to help you. Jesus taught us in John 14 and 16 that the Father sent the Holy Spirit to help us in all things. He is a great tutor. Invite Him to lead you and speak to you today. Jesus said the Holy Spirit "will tell you things to come" (John 16:13).The Holy Spirit will help you pass God's tests.

NOTES:

PSALM 12
NEW KING JAMES VERSION

¹ *Help, LORD, for the godly man ceases!*
For the faithful disappear from among the sons of men.
² *They speak idly everyone with his neighbor;*
With flattering lips and a double heart they speak.

³ *May the LORD cut off all flattering lips,*
And the tongue that speaks proud things,
⁴ *Who have said,*
"With our tongue we will prevail;
Our lips are our own;
Who is lord over us?"

⁵ *"For the oppression of the poor, for the sighing of the needy,*
Now I will arise," says the LORD;
"I will set him in the safety for which he yearns."

⁶ *The words of the LORD are pure words,*
Like silver tried in a furnace of earth,
Purified seven times.
⁷ *You shall keep them, O LORD,*
You shall preserve them from this generation forever.

⁸ *The wicked prowl on every side,*
When vileness is exalted among the sons of men.

10

THUNDER
PSALM 12

The tongue, mentioned quite often in Scripture, is a key theme in this psalm. God's Word gives warnings and admonitions regarding the tongue because it is so hard to control and tame. In James 3, the writer used the image of a horse to illustrate control of the tongue (James 3:3-8). Horses are such powerful animals that only an expert can tame them.

My family had horses when I was a boy, which allowed me to see the brute strength of these beautiful animals. In addition to their strength, horses are very smart creatures. They know when someone who climbs on their back is incapable of handling them. I have observed that on a first-hand basis. My brother had a horse that was appropriately named Thunder. One day, a family friend begged to ride him. The moment she hit the saddle, Thunder took off. Needless to say, she didn't last long on his back. Thunder knew he was in control with this rider.

Thunder was a controllable horse, but he was not tame. When I think of a "tame" horse, I think of one at the county fair walking in circles that anyone can ride. To say anyone could easily "control" Thunder would be a great stretch of the imagination. There is a difference between the words "control" and "tame." My brother could easily control Thunder. As a good horseman, he knew Thunder's personality, characteristics, and limits.

As the "horseman" of your tongue, you need to be aware of its limits. Ask God to help you control your tongue and guide your speech. The tongue is loaded with power – it can heal or kill, build up or tear down. Proverbs 18:21 says, "Death and life are in the power of the tongue." The choice is ours. Proverbs 21:23 says, "Whoever guards his mouth and tongue keeps his soul from troubles." Because God knows the power of our words, He will help us control our tongue.

Although James says we cannot "tame" our tongue, we can control it. The Psalmist David says the ungodly and unfaithful man speaks with a "double heart," which means "an inconsistent mind" (Psalm 12:1, 2). In other words, they just say anything that strikes them. That is a recipe for trouble. We must learn to be consistent in this area and guard against double-mindedness. James 1:8 declares that the "double-minded man is unstable in all his ways."

To learn how to control your tongue, you must first realize its power. Meditate on Psalm 12:6, which says, "The words of the Lord are pure words, like silver tried in a furnace of earth, purified seven times." (See also Psalm 19:7-10.) The one sure way to speak words of health, life, peace, and joy is to speak words that God would speak or agree with. His Word is pure and has the power of thunder.

NOTES:

PSALM 13
NEW KING JAMES VERSION

---

[1] *How long, O LORD? Will You forget me forever?*
How long will You hide Your face from me?
[2] *How long shall I take counsel in my soul,*
Having sorrow in my heart daily?
How long will my enemy be exalted over me?

[3] *Consider and hear me, O LORD my God;*
Enlighten my eyes,
Lest I sleep the sleep of death;
[4] *Lest my enemy say,*
"I have prevailed against him";
Lest those who trouble me rejoice when I am moved.

[5] *But I have trusted in Your mercy;*
My heart shall rejoice in Your salvation.
[6] *I will sing to the LORD,*
Because He has dealt bountifully with me.

11
I CAN SEE CLEARLY NOW
PSALM 13

Christian artist Geoff Moore recorded an old song written by Johnny Nash entitled "I Can See Clearly Now." It goes like this:

I can see clearly now, the rain is gone,
I can see all obstacles in my way
Gone are the dark clouds that had me blind
It's gonna be a bright (bright), bright (bright)
Sunshiny day.

In Psalm 13:3 David prayed, "Consider and hear me, O Lord my God; enlighten my eyes." He was praying for God to remove the darkness obscuring his path. Although David couldn't see "all the obstacles in his way," he knew God saw what lay ahead of him.

If you are like David and need some clarity along life's path, pray for God to remove all hidden things of darkness. David had people who were secretly plotting against him. As they plotted, David was in the dark, but God was watching every plan they made. God wants to reveal hidden things to those who are devoted to Him.

One place to go for enlightenment is God's Word. Psalm 119:130 says, "The entrance of Your words gives light; it gives understanding to the simple." If you have ever walked a dark path on a moonless night, you know what a huge difference one little flashlight can make. God's Word is the light when the path grows dark.

In Psalm 13, the word "enlighten" means to "restore the sparkle in one's eye." When I first went to the former Soviet Union in the early 1990's, most people had no sparkle in their eyes. Their eyes screamed hopelessness and despair. When the wall separating the USSR from the outside world came down, there was a season of opportunity to take the Gospel freely into every corner of that nation. Our family had the privilege of seeing the light come into the eyes of numerous people as they received the Good News of the Gospel. A few days ago, we had coffee with our first convert from the Ukraine, Victor Oleynik and his wife Galla. The sparkle remains in their eyes fifteen years later.

God will remove the darkness and uncertainty that may surround you, and He can put a sparkle in your eye and a spring in your step. As you meditate on this psalm today, pray for God to enlighten your eyes. Then, try singing it like Geoff Moore, "I can see clearly now...."

NOTES:

PSALM 14
NEW KING JAMES VERSION

---

[1] The fool has said in his heart,
"There is no God."
They are corrupt,
They have done abominable works,
There is none who does good.

[2] The LORD looks down from heaven upon the children of men,
To see if there are any who understand, who seek God.
[3] They have all turned aside,
They have together become corrupt;
There is none who does good,
No, not one.

[4] Have all the workers of iniquity no knowledge,
Who eat up my people as they eat bread,
And do not call on the LORD?
[5] There they are in great fear,
For God is with the generation of the righteous.
[6] You shame the counsel of the poor,
But the LORD is his refuge.

[7] Oh, that the salvation of Israel would come out of Zion!
When the LORD brings back the captivity of His people,
Let Jacob rejoice and Israel be glad.

12

FOOLS TALK
PSALM 14

In Psalm 14, David described how fools talk. Verse 1 calls someone who denies the existence of God a foolish person. Verse 4 says those with "no knowledge…do not call on the Lord." Obviously, this is not a camp you would want to associate with!

As Christians, we obviously believe in the existence of God. But is it possible we ignore Him at times? We may never do it intentionally, but it's far too easy in our busy society to go days on end without talking to Him. Don't be guilty of this. On days you are running late and have no time remaining for morning prayer, you can still prevent yourself from ignoring God. While you are driving to work, turn off the radio and talk to Him. The morning and evening commute are excellent opportunities to spend a few moments worshipping the Lord.

The Apostle Paul admonished us to "pray without ceasing" (1Thessalonians 5:17). It's important for you to acknowledge God throughout your day. If it helps, write a little note in your planner or desktop calendar to remind you to acknowledge the Lord during your day.

Have you ever sat in a room with someone who would not talk to you? They treat you as if you do not exist. According to Psalm 14:1, "The fool says in his heart, 'There is no God.'" I would never verbally deny the existence of God, and I don't want to be guilty of denying Him through my actions either. Actions often speak louder than words.

God's Word teaches that He is always with us. Because my heart is convinced of this truth, I want my actions to confirm my belief as well. I do not want to be guilty of ignoring Him.

God makes it easy for us to connect with Him. Psalm 14:2 says, "The Lord looks down from heaven upon the children of men, to see if there are any who understand, who seek God." God is looking for people to seek Him, and He guarantees to be found by those who are looking for Him with all their heart.

NOTES:

PSALM 15
NEW KING JAMES VERSION

¹ LORD, who may abide in Your tabernacle?
Who may dwell in Your holy hill?

² He who walks uprightly,
And works righteousness,
And speaks the truth in his heart;
³ He who does not backbite with his tongue,
Nor does evil to his neighbor,
Nor does he take up a reproach against his friend;
⁴ In whose eyes a vile person is despised,
But he honors those who fear the LORD;
He who swears to his own hurt and does not change;
⁵ He who does not put out his money at usury,
Nor does he take a bribe against the innocent.

He who does these things shall never be moved.

13

I WANT TO LIVE IN A BIG HOUSE
PSALM 15

Psalm 15, one of the greatest teachings on character, details the character of those who may dwell with the Lord. The psalmist asks, "Lord, who may abide in Your tabernacle? Who may dwell in Your holy hill?" David then answers his own question. The "dwellers" are those who:

- Walk uprightly and work righteousness (15:2)
- Speak the truth in their heart; are honest with themselves and meditate the Word (15:2)
- Do no evil to another, by deed or word (15:3)
- Despise evildoers and honor those who fear the Lord (15:4)
- Keep God's Word (15:4)
- Do not take advantage of others, especially the needy (15:5)

Those may sound like lofty goals, but the reward is immeasurable. The outcome is worth the effort. Of course, you cannot meet these standards on your own. Christ dwelling in you is the only thing that will enable you to live uprightly. Within ourselves, we don't measure up, but with Him, we are capable of living up to the standard.

Christians have the awesome privilege of living with the Lord eternally. God's house is big! I don't know about you, but I sure want to live in a big house. Jesus said in John 14:2, "In my Father's house are many mansions; if it were not so, I would have told you. I go to prepare a place for you." Think about how big the Father's house is. We often think of it as a mansion, but notice what Jesus said: "In my Father's house are many mansions." The Father's house has many mansions in it! Although my mind cannot comprehend the immensity of the Father's house, I want to live there. I couldn't get there on my own, but Jesus made a way.

After we have confessed Jesus Christ as Savior, we should focus on building these character qualities mentioned in Psalm 15. You will not be perfect, but put forth the effort and ask the Holy Spirit to help you grow. Jesus has gone ahead of you and has a place prepared for you to live. Once you get there, you will never move again. Won't that be wonderful?

NOTES:

PSALM 16
NEW KING JAMES VERSION

¹ Preserve me, O God, for in You I put my trust.

² O my soul, you have said to the LORD,
"You are my Lord,
My goodness is nothing apart from You."
³ As for the saints who are on the earth,
"They are the excellent ones, in whom is all my delight."

⁴ Their sorrows shall be multiplied who hasten after another god;
Their drink offerings of blood I will not offer,
Nor take up their names on my lips.

⁵ O LORD, You are the portion of my inheritance and my cup;
You maintain my lot.
⁶ The lines have fallen to me in pleasant places;
Yes, I have a good inheritance.

⁷ I will bless the LORD who has given me counsel;
My heart also instructs me in the night seasons.
⁸ I have set the LORD always before me;
Because He is at my right hand I shall not be moved.

⁹ Therefore my heart is glad, and my glory rejoices;
My flesh also will rest in hope.
¹⁰ For You will not leave my soul in Sheol,
Nor will You allow Your Holy One to see corruption.
¹¹ You will show me the path of life;
In Your presence is fullness of joy;
At Your right hand are pleasures forevermore.

14
RIGHT HAND BENEFITS
PSALM 16

One of my favorite verses in the Psalms is Psalm 16:11: "You will show me the path of life; In Your presence is fullness of joy; At Your right hand are pleasures forevermore." Today, I would like to focus on the three key principles found in this verse.

"You will show me the path of life." The path of life can be full of surprises. As a child, I dreamed of being a dentist. When asked what I wanted to be when I grew up, I always replied "a dentist." It was many years before I figured out I would not spend my life filling cavities.

Most of us have at one time or another thought life's path would go one way, but in the end, God had another path. I have no doubt Pam and I are on the path God chose for us. We have spent our entire adult lives in fulltime ministry. However, I recently said, "If you had told me fifteen years ago God would have us so heavily involved in humanitarian relief along with the other aspects of ministry He has called us to, I would have thought you had no idea what you were talking about." I had no idea back then that humanitarian relief was part of the path God had chosen for us.

It is very important to keep God's dreams alive in our hearts while not having tunnel vision at the same time. The path God has for you may be broader than you think. Ask God to show you the path of life, even when you are in your twilight years. Many successful businesses were started by people in their 60's and 70's. Colonel Sanders of Kentucky Fried Chicken is a good example. God's dreams for your path are bigger than yours or mine.

"In Your presence is fullness of joy." Life can sap your joy if you allow it. That is not God's plan. Don't allow the difficult moments of life to steal your joy. To prevent losing joy in the middle of rough waters, learn to abide in God's presence. The Bible says God inhabits the praises of His people. When those joy-stealing events occur, stop and praise God. First Thessalonians 5:18 admonishes us to give thanks in everything "for this is the will of God in Christ Jesus for you." Although God is always with you, you will become more aware of His presence by developing a lifestyle of praise.

"At Your right hand are pleasures forevermore." That is what I call "right hand benefits." This psalm was written about 1,000 years before Christ. After Jesus died and rose again, He sat down at the right hand of God. (See Mark 14:62; Acts 7:55; Heb. 10:12.) Real pleasure in life does not come from material things. God is not against His people having material possessions as long as they do not become their focus.

Earthly pleasures are only temporary. If you want to know true pleasure in life, look at God's right hand. That is where you will find "pleasures forevermore." True pleasure comes from the peace, contentment, security, and joy that flow out of a personal relationship with the Son of God. He is not positioned on God's right hand solely for a place to wait until He returns. Hebrews 7:25 says, "He is also able to save to the uttermost those who come to God through Him, since He always lives to make intercession for them." We can only come to God through Jesus, for He is the way, the Truth, and the life! (See John 14:6.) He is the way to "pleasures forevermore."

NOTES:

PSALM 17
NEW KING JAMES VERSION

¹ Hear a just cause, O LORD,
Attend to my cry;
Give ear to my prayer which is not from deceitful lips.
² Let my vindication come from Your presence;
Let Your eyes look on the things that are upright.

³ You have tested my heart;
You have visited me in the night;
You have tried me and have found nothing;
I have purposed that my mouth shall not transgress.
⁴ Concerning the works of men,
By the word of Your lips,
I have kept away from the paths of the destroyer.
⁵ Uphold my steps in Your paths,
That my footsteps may not slip.

⁶ I have called upon You, for You will hear me, O God;
Incline Your ear to me, and hear my speech.
⁷ Show Your marvelous lovingkindness by Your right hand,
O You who save those who trust in You
From those who rise up against them.
⁸ Keep me as the apple of Your eye;
Hide me under the shadow of Your wings,
⁹ From the wicked who oppress me,
From my deadly enemies who surround me.

¹⁰ They have closed up their fat hearts;
With their mouths they speak proudly.
¹¹ They have now surrounded us in our steps;
They have set their eyes, crouching down to the earth,
¹² As a lion is eager to tear his prey,
And like a young lion lurking in secret places.

¹³ Arise, O LORD,
Confront him, cast him down;
Deliver my life from the wicked with Your sword,
¹⁴ With Your hand from men, O LORD,

From men of the world who have their portion in this life,
And whose belly You fill with Your hidden treasure.
They are satisfied with children,
And leave the rest of their possession for their babes.

[15] *As for me, I will see Your face in righteousness;*
I shall be satisfied when I awake in Your likeness.

15

APPLE OF YOUR EYE
PSALM 17

Eyesight is a precious gift. I have been blessed with good eyesight, but the past few years I have become more dependent on reading glasses. If conditions are not perfect (by that I mean big print and bright light), I have a hard time reading.

I recently took my 80-year-old father to the eye doctor for a checkup. Since it had been years since he'd had an eye exam, I was certain the doctor would quickly make major adjustments to his lenses. To my surprise, the doctor declared, "He has great eyesight. He will never have to worry about going blind." How blessed my father is for that. Recently, I have had many friends past the age of fifty make a comment to me about their eyes. Eyesight is definitely a treasured blessing from God.

In Psalm 17:8, David prayed, "Keep me as the apple of Your eye." That is a phrase we have heard many times, but David prayed for it. The phrase "apple of your eye" is drawn from Deuteronomy 32:10. God found Israel "in a desert land and in the wasteland, a howling wilderness; He encircled him, He instructed him, He kept him as the apple of His eye." The Hebrew word for "apple" is *ishon* which means the "dark pupil of the eye." It also means "the hole, door, or gate of the eye."

Because sight is so greatly cherished, we are careful to preserve and protect it. To preserve the preciousness of sight was the main reason I took my father to the eye doctor. In keeping us as the apple of His eye, God is diligently protecting and cherishing us. There is daily comfort in knowing He unconditionally loves us and protects us. God's people are the apple of His eye.

Now, here comes the real question. What is the apple of your eye? The Bible talks about what should be the apple of your eye. Proverbs 7:1, 2 says, "My son, keep my words, and treasure my commands within you. Keep my commands and live, and my law as the apple of your eye." In addition to being the apple of God's eye, we are to keep the Word of God as the apple of our eye.

These two "apples" will keep us in a secure place. The first apple is our being the apple of God's eye. That covers everything externally. God diligently watches over those He loves to defend and protect from all harm and evil. The second apple will keep us in a secure place internally. As the apple of our eye, God's Word sets guard over our heart, our thoughts, and our attitude. With these two apples in place, our lives will be protected and preserved.

PSALM 18
THE MESSAGE BIBLE

1-2 I love you, God— you make me strong.
God is bedrock under my feet,
the castle in which I live,
my rescuing knight.
My God—the high crag
where I run for dear life,
hiding behind the boulders,
safe in the granite hideout.

3 I sing to God, the Praise-Lofty,
and find myself safe and saved.

20-24 God made my life complete
when I placed all the pieces before him.
When I got my act together,
he gave me a fresh start.
Now I'm alert to God's ways;
I don't take God for granted.
Every day I review the ways he works;
I try not to miss a trick.
I feel put back together,
and I'm watching my step.
God rewrote the text of my life
when I opened the book of my heart to his eyes.

16
HUMPTY DUMPTY
PSALM 18

We all know the Humpty Dumpty story from childhood: "All of the king's horses and all of the king's men couldn't put Humpty together again." Humpty was shattered and broken, and man could not help. Sound familiar?

Sin has broken all of our lives at one time or another. We all have sinned (Romans 3:23). No other person could do anything about the price of our sin. Thank God He sent Jesus to put us back together again.

Notice Psalm 18:20-24 from The Message Bible. David wrote this after he was delivered from Saul and all his enemies: "God made my life complete when I placed all the pieces before Him. When I got my act together, He gave me a fresh start. Now I'm alert to God's ways; I don't take God for granted. Every day I review the ways He works; I try not to miss a trick. I feel put back together, and I'm watching my step. God rewrote the text of my life when I opened the book of my heart to His eyes."

When did God make David's life complete? It was only after he placed "all the pieces" before Him. You cannot hold on to anything and expect God to make your life complete. The joy of Christianity is only experienced when one makes a full surrender of his life to Christ.

Notice David's honesty in this psalm: "When I got my act together, He gave me a fresh start." David laid aside all self-sufficiency and totally relied on God. He got himself out of God's way and let God be in charge of his life. If any of this describes your current condition, please do what David did, recorded in verse 24: "I opened the book of my heart to His eyes." Open up to God, call upon Him, and He will gently come near.

After opening your heart and life to Him, make a decision as did David to "review the way He works" every day. Try not to "miss a trick" – don't miss out on anything God has for you. Emulate David when he said, "I am watching my step." The end result of such submission and caution is priceless. David went on to say, "I feel put back together again" because "God rewrote the text of my life." God gave him a new start, wiping out the past and creating a future better than David could ever dream. Unlike the Humpty Dumpty story, the King was able to restore David. As you meditate on this psalm today, open your heart to the Lord and, if needed, allow Him to "put you back together again."

NOTES:

PSALM 19
NEW KING JAMES VERSION

*[1] The heavens declare the glory of God;
And the firmament shows His handiwork.
[2] Day unto day utters speech,
And night unto night reveals knowledge.
[3] There is no speech nor language
Where their voice is not heard.
[4] Their line has gone out through all the earth,
And their words to the end of the world.
In them He has set a tabernacle for the sun,
[5] Which is like a bridegroom coming out of his chamber,
And rejoices like a strong man to run its race.
[6] Its rising is from one end of heaven,
And its circuit to the other end;
And there is nothing hidden from its heat.
[7] The law of the LORD is perfect, converting the soul;
The testimony of the LORD is sure, making wise the simple;
[8] The statutes of the LORD are right, rejoicing the heart;
The commandment of the LORD is pure, enlightening the eyes;
[9] The fear of the LORD is clean, enduring forever;
The judgments of the LORD are true and righteous altogether.
[10] More to be desired are they than gold,
Yea, than much fine gold;
Sweeter also than honey and the honeycomb.
[11] Moreover by them Your servant is warned,
And in keeping them there is great reward.
[12] Who can understand his errors?
Cleanse me from secret faults.
[13] Keep back Your servant also from presumptuous sins;
Let them not have dominion over me.
Then I shall be blameless,
And I shall be innocent of great transgression.
[14] Let the words of my mouth and the meditation of my heart
Be acceptable in Your sight,
O LORD, my strength and my Redeemer.*

17

THE SECRET IS OUT
PSALM 19

Psalm 19 beautifully unites the two ways God has revealed Himself to man – by general revelation in His creation (Psalm 19:1-6; Romans 1:19, 20) and by specific revelation in His inspired Word (Psalm 19:7-14; Hebrews 1:1). God reveals Himself and clearly points the way to live submitted to His authority.

This psalm is largely responsible for my writing this devotional. In the foreword, I mentioned how the Lord directed me to meditate the Psalms of David in my devotions. During one of the first mornings I was meditating David's Psalms, I chose Psalm 19. At that time I was not studying them in sequential order. I came to verses 12 and 13, which say, "Who can understand his errors? Cleanse me from secret faults. Keep back Your servant also from presumptuous sins; let them not have dominion over me. Then I shall be blameless, and I shall be innocent of great (much) transgression." I had always viewed secret faults as sins committed in secret that no one else knew, and presumptuous sins as those committed openly or intentionally. My view, whether right or wrong, was not what God wanted to talk to me about.

As I was meditating on the phrase "secret faults," I heard the Lord whisper to my spirit, "What about faults you have that are a secret to you?" His question surprised me. I had never before thought of it like that. I said, "Lord, what are you talking about?" In reply, He showed me that I had been selfish with my wife. I had not realized that, but as soon as He pointed it out, I immediately saw where I had been self-centered. When I asked Pam about it, she was gracious. She had noticed my selfish ways,

73

but never said anything. I quickly asked her and the Lord to forgive me.

After the Lord made me aware of my selfishness, I was accountable and had a decision to make. A response of repentance gave me two great benefits: a closer, intimate relationship with the Lord and with my wife. I could then understand the meaning of David's question at the start of verse 12: "Who can understand his errors?" Only with the help of the Holy Spirit could I understand my error of selfishness toward my wife. I am grateful He loves me enough to correct me (Hebrews 12:6, 7).

I am convinced all of us have secret faults. You might call them blind spots. Dealing properly with sin and secret faults involves the courage to allow the Word of God and the Holy Spirit to examine our hearts and minds. I would like to encourage you to pray as David did. Have the courage to ask the Lord to reveal and cleanse any secret faults. Secret faults may be those you do not see but everyone else does. Ask the Lord to reveal them, so you can repent of them. God's gracious forgiveness will cover all.

NOTES:

PSALM 20
NEW KING JAMES VERSION

¹ May the LORD answer you in the day of trouble;
May the name of the God of Jacob defend you;
² May He send you help from the sanctuary,
And strengthen you out of Zion;
³ May He remember all your offerings,
And accept your burnt sacrifice. Selah

⁴ May He grant you according to your heart's desire,
And fulfill all your purpose.
⁵ We will rejoice in your salvation,
And in the name of our God we will set up our banners!
May the LORD fulfill all your petitions.

⁶ Now I know that the LORD saves His anointed;
He will answer him from His holy heaven
With the saving strength of His right hand.

⁷ Some trust in chariots, and some in horses;
But we will remember the name of the LORD our God.
⁸ They have bowed down and fallen;
But we have risen and stand upright.

⁹ Save, LORD!
May the King answer us when we call.

18
HE TOOK OFF THEIR CHARIOT WHEELS
PSALM 20

Some primitive tribes believe that calling out the name of a chief or person of rank and power can bring protection. David said in Psalm 20:1: "May the name of the God of Jacob defend you." In verse 7 he said, "We will remember the name of the Lord our God." David knew that calling on the name of the Lord invokes His power over powerful foes. His name is above all other names!

In David's time, many nations that were hostile towards Israel had mighty armies equipped with horses and chariots. Chariots were a stately symbol of power, especially to the soldier resigned to battle on foot. Chariots provided the advantage of protection and speed to the charioteer. However, the charioteer was not invulnerable to a wiser opponent.

Did you ever see the movie *Gladiators*? The main character, played by Russell Crowe, was forced to be a gladiator in Rome. Bloodthirsty crowds watched these men fight one another until death. In the movie, there's a scene where Crowe and his men are in the coliseum while the chariots begin to advance upon them. It looks hopeless until the gladiators form a protective circle with their shields, creating a ramp that throws the chariot off balance, causing it to topple over. This allowed Crowe's team to overcome the charioteers.

David understood that the most powerful and well-equipped armies were no match for those who put their trust in the name of the Lord. That is why he declared in Psalm 20:7: "Some trust in chariots, and some in horses; but we will remember the name of the Lord our God." If it seems like horses and chariots are coming at you, remember the name of the Lord your God. He will defend you.

A great example of God's delivering power is found in Exodus 14. The Israelites had been enslaved in Egypt for over 400 years. God sent Moses to lead them to freedom, but it appeared Moses had led them in the wrong way. The Israelites became trapped – on one side was the Red Sea and on the other was Pharaoh with "six hundred choice chariots and all the chariots of Egypt." Pharaoh's intent was to capture them and bring them back into slavery.

Upon hearing the cries of the people, Moses declared, "Do not be afraid. Stand still and see the salvation of the Lord, which He will accomplish for you today....The Lord will fight for you" (Exodus 14:13,14). God then parted the Red Sea, and the Israelites walked across on dry ground. However, the chariots were still in hot pursuit of the Israelites. Without a miracle, the people were doomed. But look what God did: "The Lord looked down upon the army of the Egyptians...and He took off their chariot wheels" (Exodus 14:24, 25).

In light of that story, it's easy to understand why David wrote Psalm 20:7. Whatever your need may be, call on the name of the Lord today. He can handle the chariots, even if he has to take off their wheels.

NOTES:

PSALM 21
NEW KING JAMES VERSION

¹ The king shall have joy in Your strength, O LORD;
And in Your salvation how greatly shall he rejoice!
² You have given him his heart's desire,
And have not withheld the request of his lips. Selah

³ For You meet him with the blessings of goodness;
You set a crown of pure gold upon his head.
⁴ He asked life from You, and You gave it to him—
Length of days forever and ever.
⁵ His glory is great in Your salvation;
Honor and majesty You have placed upon him.
⁶ For You have made him most blessed forever;
You have made him exceedingly glad with Your presence.
⁷ For the king trusts in the LORD,
And through the mercy of the Most High he shall not be moved.

⁸ Your hand will find all Your enemies;
Your right hand will find those who hate You.
⁹ You shall make them as a fiery oven in the time of Your anger;
The LORD shall swallow them up in His wrath,
And the fire shall devour them.
¹⁰ Their offspring You shall destroy from the earth,
And their descendants from among the sons of men.
¹¹ For they intended evil against You;
They devised a plot which they are not able to perform.
¹² Therefore You will make them turn their back;
You will make ready Your arrows on Your string toward their faces.

¹³ Be exalted, O LORD, in Your own strength!
We will sing and praise Your power.

19

NO SWEAT
PSALM 21

Many Bible commentators, as well as Jewish rabbis, see this psalm in two parts. The first part (verses 1-7) generally refers to David, while the second part prophesies of a coming king (Jesus) ascending in victory. The psalm is a thankful praise for victory. David said in verse 3, "You set a crown of pure gold upon his head." After victory over the Ammonites in 2 Samuel 12:30, David received the royal crown of the conquered king. This was a powerful symbol of victory over his foe.

What battles can you look back over in your life and see where the Lord gave you the victory? It is so easy to focus on the challenges at hand and forget that He has always been faithful. Yet, remembering the past faithfulness of God has been the catalyst to my faith today. I may not be able to look ahead and see how well things will turn out, but I have a good memory. I remember the many times God has seen me through a challenge. He has not changed.

As mentioned earlier, this psalm is basically divided into two parts. In the first part of the psalm, David looked back and saw the past faithfulness of God during his life and rule. The second part is prophetic. Prophecy foretells, or it tells something before it happens. Verse 9 refers to Christ, a descendant of David: "You shall make them (Messiah's enemies) as a fiery oven in the time of Your anger." God's judgment is often described as fire (Malachi 4:1), and it will be the means of bringing the final Judgment Day to a conclusion (2 Peter 3:7).

By looking back at the faithfulness of God while looking forward to the fulfillment of God's promises, David was able to stay consistent in his life. Because he understood the character of God, he was able to put his trust in God's ability to take care of both his present and future troubles. He knew victory belonged to him in his past, his present, and his future.

The enemy in front of you always looks a lot bigger than the one behind you. That's why it's important to keep looking at past victories when faced with a great battle. In David's case, he killed a lion and a bear before he ever encountered Goliath. By the time Goliath showed up, he didn't look so big. Since he had already killed a lion and a bear in the past, defeating Goliath was no sweat. If something looks big in front of you today, look back first. After that, when you turn around and look at what is in front of you, it will not look so big. The same God who showed up in the past is in your present and future!

NOTES:

PSALM 22
NEW KING JAMES VERSION

¹ My God, My God, why have You forsaken Me?
Why are You so far from helping Me,
And from the words of My groaning?
² O My God, I cry in the daytime, but You do not hear;
And in the night season, and am not silent.

³ But You are holy,
Enthroned in the praises of Israel.
⁴ Our fathers trusted in You;
They trusted, and You delivered them.
⁵ They cried to You, and were delivered;
They trusted in You, and were not ashamed.

⁶ But I am a worm, and no man;
A reproach of men, and despised by the people.
⁷ All those who see Me ridicule Me;
They shoot out the lip, they shake the head, saying,
⁸ "He trusted in the LORD, let Him rescue Him;
Let Him deliver Him, since He delights in Him!"

⁹ But You are He who took Me out of the womb;
You made Me trust while on My mother's breasts.
¹⁰ I was cast upon You from birth.
From My mother's womb
You have been My God.
¹¹ Be not far from Me,
For trouble is near;
For there is none to help.

¹² Many bulls have surrounded Me;
Strong bulls of Bashan have encircled Me.
¹³ They gape at Me with their mouths,
Like a raging and roaring lion.

¹⁴ I am poured out like water,
And all My bones are out of joint;
My heart is like wax;
It has melted within Me.
¹⁵ My strength is dried up like a potsherd,
And My tongue clings to My jaws;
You have brought Me to the dust of death.

¹⁶ For dogs have surrounded Me;
The congregation of the wicked has enclosed Me.
They pierced My hands and My feet;
¹⁷ I can count all My bones.
They look and stare at Me.
¹⁸ They divide My garments among them,
And for My clothing they cast lots.

¹⁹ But You, O LORD, do not be far from Me;
O My Strength, hasten to help Me!
²⁰ Deliver Me from the sword,
My precious life from the power of the dog.
²¹ Save Me from the lion's mouth
And from the horns of the wild oxen!

You have answered Me.

²² I will declare Your name to My brethren;
In the midst of the assembly I will praise You.
²³ You who fear the LORD, praise Him!
All you descendants of Jacob, glorify Him,
And fear Him, all you offspring of Israel!
²⁴ For He has not despised nor abhorred
the affliction of the afflicted;
Nor has He hidden His face from Him;
But when He cried to Him, He heard.

²⁵ My praise shall be of You in the great assembly;
I will pay My vows before those who fear Him.
²⁶ The poor shall eat and be satisfied;
Those who seek Him will praise the LORD.

Let your heart live forever!

²⁷ All the ends of the world
Shall remember and turn to the LORD,
And all the families of the nations
Shall worship before You.
²⁸ For the kingdom is the LORD's,
And He rules over the nations.

²⁹ All the prosperous of the earth
Shall eat and worship;
All those who go down to the dust
Shall bow before Him,
Even he who cannot keep himself alive.

³⁰ A posterity shall serve Him.
It will be recounted of the Lord to the next generation,
³¹ They will come and declare His
righteousness to a people who will be born,
That He has done this.

20

SING, MOMMA, SING
PSALM 22

Years ago, the Lord miraculously healed my wife, Pam. I'll tell the story in more detail later in this book (Psalm 108 devotion), but for now, suffice it to say she had been seriously ill for four years. At times, she would be so sick that she couldn't even keep water in her stomach. She would become dehydrated and sometimes have to be hospitalized. During these bouts, she would experience excruciating abdominal pain. As a husband, I felt helpless, as there was nothing I could do to relieve the pain.

During one of these bouts, Pam's mother was in our home. Pam was in horrific pain. We had prayed every prayer we knew to pray. Finally, her mother began to sing to the Lord. When she stopped singing, Pam, in her weak voice said, "Sing, Momma, Sing." When her mother sang, the pain subsided. When she stopped, the pain returned. I do not have a theological answer for this. I just know that when her mother sang to the Lord, the pain left. The Bible does tell us that God inhabits the praises of His people.

Bible scholars say Psalm 22 is a prophetic psalm describing the suffering, praise, and posterity of the Messiah. David began this psalm by saying, "My God, My God, why have You forsaken me?" Matthew 27:46 records Christ saying the same words as He was crucified. Perhaps David felt forsaken at the time he penned this psalm. Maybe some of you have felt that way as well.

But one thing is for certain: God has never, and will never, forsake any of us. Of course during Pam's illness, there were times the question arose, "God, do you hear me?" These questions are questions of doubt, not faith. We do not want to feed those questions; we want to feed our faith. Meditate something from this psalm today because "faith comes by hearing, and hearing by the Word of God."

David did not stop with his question of doubt. He went on to describe the unpleasant reality of suffering. However, he didn't end there either. In the last several verses of the psalm, David declared the end result of the Messiah's redemptive work. As children of God, we are under the umbrella of His provision.

Because God has already redeemed us, we can have a note of praise throughout the day. I'll never forget Pam's words, "Sing, Momma, sing." If you experience something painful, remember those words. They will remind you to sing praises to God. As you praise Him, He will appear larger and your problems smaller. If you need encouragement, do as David did in verses 4 and 5. He remembered the times God had shown Himself faithful. God's nature never changes – if He was faithful in the past, He will be faithful in the future. So take time to think upon God's faithfulness and praise Him today!

NOTES:

Psalm 23
New King James Version

¹ The LORD is my shepherd;
I shall not want.
² He makes me to lie down in green pastures;
He leads me beside the still waters.
³ He restores my soul;
He leads me in the paths of righteousness
For His name's sake.

⁴ Yea, though I walk through the valley of the shadow of death,
I will fear no evil;
For You are with me;
Your rod and Your staff, they comfort me.

⁵ You prepare a table before me in the presence of my enemies;
You anoint my head with oil;
My cup runs over.
⁶ Surely goodness and mercy shall follow me
All the days of my life;
And I will dwell in the house of the LORD
Forever.

21

BLOODHOUNDS
PSALM 23

David's first psalm, Psalm 23, was probably written shortly after he was anointed to be king while he was still keeping his father's flocks in Bethlehem. In this famous psalm, we tend to focus on the theme of the shepherd. I would like to focus on "bloodhounds" instead.

A bloodhound is a special breed of dog with an uncanny ability to track. These dogs are often used in law enforcement when someone lost or in hiding needs to be found. When a bloodhound smells the scent of the missing person, he takes off following the scent trail. Bloodhounds are hard to shake. Once they get on track of a scent, it is almost impossible to get their attention anywhere else. They are very determined animals and don't give up on a scent until they find it. Because their olfactory senses are so phenomenal, they can find their prey just about anywhere.

In Psalm 23, there are two bloodhounds named "goodness and mercy." David said in verse 6, "Surely goodness and mercy shall follow me all the days of my life." He left no doubt about it – goodness and mercy "shall follow me." Just like it is nearly impossible to get away from a bloodhound, God's people cannot escape His goodness and mercy. They will track you down! They have a determined assignment from God to follow you. Like a bloodhound, you may not even know they are on your trail.

Life in Christ is more enjoyable when we acknowledge these two determined trackers. No matter where life's path leads you, you cannot shake them. I have been around some miserable people who were believers. All they can focus on is temporal problems or things that did not go the way they had planned. But don't let those delays or unexpected situations steal your joy. What God's goodness and mercy have done for you is so much more important than any temporal circumstance.

Every day I breathe, I am receiving the goodness of God. His goodness and mercy track me down. In God's goodness, He has made a way for me through His mercy to escape eternal damnation. It doesn't get much better than that.

After David wrote this psalm, he had many opportunities to be discouraged with events in life. He made up his mind early on, declaring in this psalm, "Though I walk through the valley of the shadow of death, I will fear no evil." Why was David unafraid of evil? Because the two bloodhounds of goodness and mercy always found a way to get to him. They tracked him down and were always with him.

Just as goodness and mercy overtook David, so will goodness and mercy track us. The Hebrew word for "mercy" is *chesed*, which means "the unfailing, steadfast covenant love of God." On the day you entered into covenant with God, through faith in Jesus Christ, His goodness and mercy locked onto you. You cannot escape them. You have already received so much of God's goodness and mercy that if you never received any more, you could never praise Him enough. Today, make this declaration as David did: "Surely goodness and mercy shall follow me all the days of my life!"

NOTES:

PSALM 24
NEW KING JAMES VERSION

¹ The earth is the LORD's, and all its fullness,
The world and those who dwell therein.
² For He has founded it upon the seas,
And established it upon the waters.

³ Who may ascend into the hill of the LORD?
Or who may stand in His holy place?
⁴ He who has clean hands and a pure heart,
Who has not lifted up his soul to an idol,
Nor sworn deceitfully.
⁵ He shall receive blessing from the LORD,
And righteousness from the God of his salvation.
⁶ This is Jacob, the generation of those who seek Him,
Who seek Your face. Selah

⁷ Lift up your heads, O you gates!
And be lifted up, you everlasting doors!
And the King of glory shall come in.
⁸ Who is this King of glory?
The LORD strong and mighty,
The LORD mighty in battle.
⁹ Lift up your heads, O you gates!
Lift up, you everlasting doors!
And the King of glory shall come in.
¹⁰ Who is this King of glory?
The LORD of hosts,
He is the King of glory.

Selah

22

JAMES BOND STUFF
PSALM 24

Have you ever answered the phone and the person on the other end immediately begins to talk thinking you know who it is? After a moment, because you did not recognize his voice, you ask, "Who is this?" When my wife calls I never have to ask, "Who is this?" Immediately, I recognize her voice. In Psalm 24, David asked twice, "Who is this King of Glory?" He went on to reveal the King so we would recognize Him.

A friend of ours owns a large security company. He recently told me that voice recognition is becoming popular in the security industry. He said it used to be only for "high-end" clients. Now it is more affordable, so it is no longer "James Bond stuff" (his exact quote). In other words, for those who need tight security, most anyone can use voice recognition.

Voice recognition is available to all. That does not sound too different from what Jesus taught in His message on the Good Shepherd. John 10:3-5 says the sheep hear the shepherd's voice "and he calls his own sheep by name and leads them out. And when he brings out his own sheep, he goes before them; and the sheep follow him, for they know his voice." Sheep hear and follow the voice of their shepherd if they recognize his voice. A good shepherd knows his sheep by name. Jesus is the Good Shepherd, and good sheep follow His voice.

The Good Shepherd has a good plan for your life (Jeremiah 29:11). You can only experience it if you hear and recognize His voice. It is extremely important that we recognize Him and His voice if we want to enjoy His Kingdom. It is also extremely important we understand that the

Word of God is His voice. The Bible is God's declared will. The words of the Good Shepherd are always in line with God's Word.

Psalm 24:1-6 is about the King of Glory and His kingdom. David described those who would dwell in the kingdom. Being "kingdom dwellers" requires knowing the desires and will of the King. And to know His desires, we must first know His voice. When we know His voice we don't ask the question "Who is this?" for we already know the answer.

The only way to recognize the Shepherd's voice is to spend time with Him. By virtue of years spent with my wife, I know her voice any time and any place. I can be in a mall with hundreds of people making noise, and I know her voice. If you have a hard time discerning the Lord's voice, don't be frustrated. Young sheep do not know their shepherd's voice at first. They just stay with him and soon learn his voice.

Today, I want to encourage you to stay with the Good Shepherd. As you continue to walk with Him, you will begin to know His voice. Spend time talking with Him every day. The Good Shepherd knows you by name and wants to show you things to come (John 16:13).

NOTES:

PSALM 25
NEW KING JAMES VERSION

¹ To You, O LORD, I lift up my soul.
² O my God, I trust in You;
Let me not be ashamed;
Let not my enemies triumph over me.
³ Indeed, let no one who waits on You be ashamed;
Let those be ashamed who deal treacherously without cause.

⁴ Show me Your ways, O LORD;
Teach me Your paths.
⁵ Lead me in Your truth and teach me,
For You are the God of my salvation;
On You I wait all the day.

⁶ Remember, O LORD, Your tender mercies and Your lovingkindnesses,
For they are from of old.
⁷ Do not remember the sins of my youth, nor my transgressions;
According to Your mercy remember me,
For Your goodness' sake, O LORD.

⁸ Good and upright is the LORD;
Therefore He teaches sinners in the way.
⁹ The humble He guides in justice,
And the humble He teaches His way.
¹⁰ All the paths of the LORD are mercy and truth,
To such as keep His covenant and His testimonies.
¹¹ For Your name's sake, O LORD,
Pardon my iniquity, for it is great.

¹² Who is the man that fears the LORD?
Him shall He teach in the way He chooses.
¹³ He himself shall dwell in prosperity,
And his descendants shall inherit the earth.
¹⁴ The secret of the LORD is with those who fear Him,
And He will show them His covenant.

15 My eyes are ever toward the LORD,
For He shall pluck my feet out of the net.

16 Turn Yourself to me, and have mercy on me,
For I am desolate and afflicted.
17 The troubles of my heart have enlarged;
Bring me out of my distresses!
18 Look on my affliction and my pain,
And forgive all my sins.
19 Consider my enemies, for they are many;
And they hate me with cruel hatred.
20 Keep my soul, and deliver me;
Let me not be ashamed, for I put my trust in You.
21 Let integrity and uprightness preserve me,
For I wait for You.

22 Redeem Israel, O God,
Out of all their troubles!

23

STUCK IN THE MIDDLE
PSALM 25

Being stuck in the middle is not as bad as it sounds. Psalm 25:5 says, "Lead me in Your truth and teach me." The Hebrew word for "truth" here is *'emet* (eh-met). It means "certainty, rightness, and trustworthiness." The word conveys a sense of dependability, firmness, and reliability. Truth is something upon which a person may confidently stake his life.

Interestingly, *'emet* is spelled with the first, middle, and last letters of the Hebrew alphabet. The rabbis concluded that truth upholds the first and the last of God's creation, and everything in between.

Jesus is truth personified. He said in John 14:6, "I am the way, the truth, and the life. No one comes to the Father except through Me." John 1:1, 2 tells us of Christ's deity, stating "In the beginning was the Word, and the Word was with God, and the Word was God. He was in the beginning with God." Jesus is the Word of God and has been since the beginning.

Christ is also in the last chapter of the Bible. In Revelation 22:12, 13 Jesus testifies to His church, "And behold, I am coming quickly, and My reward is with Me, to give to everyone according to his work. I am the Alpha and the Omega, the Beginning and the End, the First and the Last." Between those two ends – the beginning of time and the end of time – is a great place to be stuck in the middle. Jesus is the Beginning, the End, and everything in between.

Jesus has everything covered. You cannot possibly experience anything to which He is not the answer. His Word is the answer to all things. His Word is Truth – it is *'emet*, the first, middle, and last letter of the alphabet. In John 17:17, Christ prayed, "Sanctify them by Your truth. Your word is truth."

Jesus also said in John 8:32, "And you shall know the truth, and the truth shall make you free." He did not say the truth will make you free, but the truth you know is what makes you free. We must know truth for its power to affect our lives.

I want to encourage you today to take a moment and memorize a Scripture. If you are in a hurry, perhaps you can write one on a card and stick it in your pocket. Then, in the middle of the day, pull it out and meditate on it. Let Jesus have a prominent place even in the middle of your day. He is the Truth 24/7 – in the beginning of the day, at its end, and all through the middle.

Psalm 26
New King James Version

¹ *Vindicate me, O LORD,*
For I have walked in my integrity.
I have also trusted in the LORD;
I shall not slip.
² *Examine me, O LORD, and prove me;*
Try my mind and my heart.
³ *For Your lovingkindness is before my eyes,*
And I have walked in Your truth.
⁴ *I have not sat with idolatrous mortals,*
Nor will I go in with hypocrites.
⁵ *I have hated the assembly of evildoers,*
And will not sit with the wicked.

⁶ *I will wash my hands in innocence;*
So I will go about Your altar, O LORD,
⁷ *That I may proclaim with the voice of thanksgiving,*
And tell of all Your wondrous works.
⁸ *LORD, I have loved the habitation of Your house,*
And the place where Your glory dwells.

⁹ *Do not gather my soul with sinners,*
Nor my life with bloodthirsty men,
¹⁰ *In whose hands is a sinister scheme,*
And whose right hand is full of bribes.

¹¹ *But as for me, I will walk in my integrity;*
Redeem me and be merciful to me.
¹² *My foot stands in an even place;*
In the congregations I will bless the LORD.

24

INTEGRITY
PSALM 26

Integrity is defined as "adherence to moral and ethical principles; soundness of moral character; honesty." Living a life of integrity was David's basis for expecting vindication. A life of integrity does not always come easy. Sometimes integrity requires making tough, painful decisions that may cost something. Integrity is extremely important. Edward R. Murrow said, "To be persuasive we must be believable; to be believable we must be credible; to be credible we must be truthful."

As we look closely at Psalm 26, we see that David was praying for divine scrutiny. In verse 2 he prayed, "Examine me, O Lord, and prove (test) me; Try my mind and my heart." David was asking God before whom nothing is hidden to examine his heart. He realized the only way to really live a life of integrity is with God's help. Man's standard of integrity may often be a lower standard than God's, because man can only look on the outside, but God looks on the heart.

First Samuel 16 records the anointing of David as king of Israel. God had made it plain to the prophet Samuel that Saul would not be allowed to remain as king. Samuel was directed by the Lord to take anointing oil and go to the home of Jesse, David's father, for the anointing of a new king.

When Samuel arrived at his destination, he arranged for an anointing service, telling Jesse to bring his sons. David's oldest brother, Eliab, was the first candidate to be presented. Verse 6 says, "So it was, when they came, that he (Samuel) looked at Eliab and said, 'Surely the Lord's anointed is before Him!'" Verse 7 says, "But the Lord said to

Samuel, 'Do not look at his appearance or at his physical stature, because I have refused him. For the Lord does not see as man sees; for man looks at the outward appearance, but the Lord looks at the heart.'"

As the story goes, all seven older brothers were presented, but God chose the youngest, David. Why did the Lord choose the seemingly most insignificant son? Because "the Lord looks at the heart." Integrity is a heart issue. That is why David prayed for God to search his heart. Only God could show him what pleased Him. Apparently, David wanted to please God more than anything or anyone else.

When walking in integrity becomes your goal, you will not slip. Psalm 26 starts with these words: "Vindicate me, O Lord, for I have walked in my integrity. I have also trusted in the Lord; I shall not slip." David knew that only God could keep him from slipping up. Let his words be your confession today: "But as for me, I will walk in my integrity; Redeem me and be merciful to me."

NOTES:

PSALM 27
NEW KING JAMES VERSION

¹ The LORD is my light and my salvation;
Whom shall I fear?
The LORD is the strength of my life;
Of whom shall I be afraid?
² When the wicked came against me
To eat up my flesh,
My enemies and foes,
They stumbled and fell.
³ Though an army may encamp against me,
My heart shall not fear;
Though war may rise against me,
In this I will be confident.

⁴ One thing I have desired of the LORD,
That will I seek:
That I may dwell in the house of the LORD
All the days of my life,
To behold the beauty of the LORD,
And to inquire in His temple.
⁵ For in the time of trouble
He shall hide me in His pavilion;
In the secret place of His tabernacle
He shall hide me;
He shall set me high upon a rock.

⁶ And now my head shall be lifted up
above my enemies all around me;
Therefore I will offer sacrifices of joy in His tabernacle;
I will sing, yes, I will sing praises to the LORD.

⁷ Hear, O LORD, when I cry with my voice!
Have mercy also upon me, and answer me.
⁸ When You said, "Seek My face,"
My heart said to You, "Your face, LORD, I will seek."

⁹ Do not hide Your face from me;
Do not turn Your servant away in anger;
You have been my help;
Do not leave me nor forsake me,
O God of my salvation.
¹⁰ When my father and my mother forsake me,
Then the LORD will take care of me.

¹¹ Teach me Your way, O LORD,
And lead me in a smooth path, because of my enemies.
¹² Do not deliver me to the will of my adversaries;
For false witnesses have risen against me,
And such as breathe out violence.
¹³ I would have lost heart, unless I had believed
That I would see the goodness of the LORD
In the land of the living.

¹⁴ Wait on the LORD;
Be of good courage,
And He shall strengthen your heart;
Wait, I say, on the LORD!

25

YOU CAN'T EAT ME
PSALM 27

A few years back, a dear friend of mine was facing a severe financial crisis in his business. Things looked hopeless, and he was pressed on every side. As I tried to encourage him, he said, "I have decided they can't eat me." That phrase may sound silly, but it actually ministered to me.

Psalm 27 is an exuberant declaration of David's faith, even as he faced the prospect of war rising against him. Pay close attention to verse 2 as you read this psalm. It says, "When the wicked came against me to eat up my flesh, my enemies and foes, they stumbled and fell." Notice David said the enemy "came." Jesus said in John 16:33, "In the world you will have tribulation; but be of good cheer, I have overcome the world." When the enemy comes, he has an agenda. In David's case, his agenda was "to eat up my flesh." The enemy may have been attacking David on all sides, but David determined the enemy would not eat him.

Human nature tends to see things worse than they really are. In this psalm, David strongly believed everything would turn out all right. In the midst of battle, he knew victory was his.

Whatever challenge you are facing is not as big as your enemy would like you to think. First Peter 5:8 says, "Your adversary the devil walks about like a roaring lion, seeking whom he may devour." Notice this verse says, "The devil walks about like a lion." The devil is not a lion; he is an imposter. His roar is worse than his bite to those who walk in faith in the power of the resurrected Christ.

Satan is aggressively hostile, much like the enemy David was describing in Psalm 27. When the "lion imposter" tries to show his teeth, the key is to maintain your confidence in the Lord. Verses 1-3 of Psalm 27 are connected. David ended verse 3 with: "In this I will be confident." In verse 1, David described the source of his confidence: "The Lord is my light and my salvation; whom shall I fear?" (The implied answer is "no one.") "The Lord is the strength of my life; of whom shall I be afraid?" (Again, the implied answer is "no one.") Because David knew his source of victory was in God, he could boldly declare, "When the wicked came against me to eat up my flesh, they couldn't eat me!" (My paraphrase.)

Finally, for anyone suffering the loss of a parent through death, divorce, or desertion, I would like to encourage you with one of David's most unique and comforting verses. It is especially interesting when one considers it was written by a man God chose to be a king. Psalm 27:10 says, "When my father and my mother forsake me, then the Lord will take care of me." You can count on God to take care of you.

PSALM 28
NEW KING JAMES VERSION

¹ To You I will cry, O LORD my Rock:
Do not be silent to me,
Lest, if You are silent to me,
I become like those who go down to the pit.
² Hear the voice of my supplications
When I cry to You,
When I lift up my hands toward Your holy sanctuary.

³ Do not take me away with the wicked
And with the workers of iniquity,
Who speak peace to their neighbors,
But evil is in their hearts.
⁴ Give them according to their deeds,
And according to the wickedness of their endeavors;
Give them according to the work of their hands;
Render to them what they deserve.
⁵ Because they do not regard the works of the LORD,
Nor the operation of His hands,
He shall destroy them
And not build them up.

⁶ Blessed be the LORD,
Because He has heard the voice of my supplications!
⁷ The LORD is my strength and my shield;
My heart trusted in Him, and I am helped;
Therefore my heart greatly rejoices,
And with my song I will praise Him.

⁸ The LORD is their strength,
And He is the saving refuge of His anointed.
⁹ Save Your people,
And bless Your inheritance;
Shepherd them also,
And bear them up forever.

26

HEART BREAK RIDGE
PSALM 28

David was obviously a man of prayer. He wrote in Psalm 28:1, 2: "To You I will cry, O Lord my Rock…Hear the voice of my supplications…" In its simplest form, prayer could be defined as communication with God. Communication is a two-way street in which both participants speak and listen to each other. In prayer, God listens to us and we listen to Him.

I once heard of a place called Heart Break Ridge in the Korean War. This ridge had a 3,000-foot ridgeline consisting of three peaks. On these peaks and in the surrounding valleys, many gruesome battles were waged, taking heavy toll on the lives of the allied and enemy forces.

At the start of an intense battle during the Korean War, one of our troops lay wounded over fifty yards from the safety of our lines. No one could get to him because of the intense incoming artillery. An officer later recounted he had noticed a young soldier consistently looking at his watch during the battle. This young soldier crawled to his fallen comrade and dragged him to safety. When the battle ended, the officer asked him why he had been looking at his watch. He replied, "Sarge, I was just waiting until it was 9:00 back home. Before I left home, my mom said she would be praying for me every day at that time. And that's when I went to rescue that soldier." I cannot vouch for the veracity of the story, but I can say it would be great for us to live with that kind of confidence in a prayer-answering God.

That soldier's mother determined to be a person of prayer. She did not foreknow that her son would be in such a predicament. She was probably praying at 9:00 on days when he was in absolutely no danger.

111

The very fact she had a consistent lifestyle of prayer was very important. When the gunfire began, it was predetermined she would pray, because she had confidence that God would keep her son safe even if thousands of miles away. We never know all of the things or reasons for which we may be praying.

First Thessalonians 5:17 admonishes us to "pray without ceasing." In order to pray, you don't have to be on your knees twenty-four hours a day. You can be driving your car to work and commune with God just like you could with anyone else in the car. I encourage you to try communicating with God frequently today. He's right there, ready to listen and speak to you.

NOTES:

PSALM 29
NEW KING JAMES VERSION

¹ *Give unto the LORD, O you mighty ones,*
Give unto the LORD glory and strength.
² *Give unto the LORD the glory due to His name;*
Worship the LORD in the beauty of holiness.

³ *The voice of the LORD is over the waters;*
The God of glory thunders;
The LORD is over many waters.
⁴ *The voice of the LORD is powerful;*
The voice of the LORD is full of majesty.

⁵ *The voice of the LORD breaks the cedars,*
Yes, the LORD splinters the cedars of Lebanon.
⁶ *He makes them also skip like a calf,*
Lebanon and Sirion like a young wild ox.
⁷ *The voice of the LORD divides the flames of fire.*

⁸ *The voice of the LORD shakes the wilderness;*
The LORD shakes the Wilderness of Kadesh.
⁹ *The voice of the LORD makes the deer give birth,*
And strips the forests bare;
And in His temple everyone says, "Glory!"

¹⁰ *The LORD sat enthroned at the Flood,*
And the LORD sits as King forever.
¹¹ *The LORD will give strength to His people;*
The LORD will bless His people with peace.

27

TAH-WA-HE
PSALM 29

Names are our primary means of identity. If I were to say your social security number to your mother and ask, "Who is this person?" she probably would not know. If I mention your name, she would know you immediately. Your name is your primary identity.

In many cultures, names are extremely meaningful. My father's name is Frank King. My father is part Osage Indian, and Tah-Wa-He is his Osage name. He has embraced his ethnicity to the point of having a naming ceremony in which he was given this Osage name. At the ceremony, the Osage official who named him said it meant "going to town." He explained it was a name of honor taken from an Osage Indian in the 1800's who was a family patriarch. It was his duty to go to town and get the supplies for the family. The name has significant meaning, which is common in many cultures.

In Psalm 29:2, David declares, "Give unto the Lord the glory due to His name..." The name of Jesus deserves honor and glory. Philippians 2:9 says, "Therefore God also has highly exalted Him and given Him the name which is above every other name, that at the name of Jesus every knee should bow, of those in heaven, and of those on earth, and of those under the earth, and that every tongue should confess that Jesus Christ is Lord, to the glory of God the Father." What a powerful name, Jesus!

The Father gave Jesus, His Son, such a name because He places emphasis on the power and importance of a name, including His own. Consider the powerful meaning of some of the names of God in the

Scriptures. They help us identify who our God is. He is all of these things and more:

El Shaddai – God All Sufficient - Genesis 17:1, 2
Jehovah-Shalom – The Lord Our Peace - Judges 6:24
Jehovah-Nissi – The Lord Our Banner - Exodus 17:15
Jehovah-Rophe – The Lord Our Healer - Exodus 15:22-26
Jehovah-Jireh – The Lord Will Provide - Genesis 22:14
Jehovah-Tsidkenu – The Lord Our Righteousness - Jeremiah 23:6

Proverbs 18:10 says, "The name of the Lord is a strong tower; the righteous run to it, and are safe." Now that is an incredible name! As you go through your day, take time to meditate on the wonderful name of Jesus. That name is a safe tower for anyone who runs to it.

NOTES:

PSALM 30
NEW KING JAMES VERSION

---

¹ I will extol You, O LORD, for You have lifted me up,
And have not let my foes rejoice over me.
² O LORD my God, I cried out to You,
And You healed me.
³ O LORD, You brought my soul up from the grave;
You have kept me alive, that I should not go down to the pit.

⁴ Sing praise to the LORD, you saints of His,
And give thanks at the remembrance of His holy name.
⁵ For His anger is but for a moment,
His favor is for life;
Weeping may endure for a night,
But joy comes in the morning.

⁶ Now in my prosperity I said,
"I shall never be moved."
⁷ LORD, by Your favor You have made
my mountain stand strong;
You hid Your face, and I was troubled.

⁸ I cried out to You, O LORD;
And to the LORD I made supplication:
⁹ "What profit is there in my blood,
When I go down to the pit?
Will the dust praise You?
Will it declare Your truth?
¹⁰ Hear, O LORD, and have mercy on me;
LORD, be my helper!"

¹¹ You have turned for me my mourning into dancing;
You have put off my sackcloth and clothed me with gladness,
¹² To the end that my glory may sing praise to You and not be silent.
O LORD my God, I will give thanks to You forever.

28

JOY IS AROUND THE CORNER
PSALM 30

Joy is one of my favorite words. It is the middle name of my wife, my daughter, and my granddaughter. Lately I have been calling my granddaughter "Little Joy." She already brings me such joy, and she won't be born for another four months! I cannot imagine the joy I'll experience when I first hold her. I will be one silly grandpa. Although all three of these girls bring me great joy, it is not comparable to the joy David referred to in Psalm 30:5. The purest joy in the world is joy only God can bring.

According to the dictionary, *joy* is "an emotion of great delight or happiness caused by something good or satisfying." The Hebrew word used here is *rinnah*, which means "a shout of rejoicing; shouting; loud cheering in triumph." It describes the kind of joyful shouting at the time of victory. If you've ever sat on the winning side at a major football game, then you have experienced *rinnah*. The word *rinnah* also means singing. In Scripture, the word is used for both joy and singing. So, Psalm 30 could read this way: "Weeping may endure for a night, but singing and loud cheering in triumph comes in the morning."

There are so many promises in this one psalm that should bring you *rinnah*. For example, the first verse says, "…You have lifted me up, and have not let my foes rejoice over me." Verse 2 says, "O Lord my God, I cried out to You, and You healed me." Verse 5 says, "His favor is for life." God's favor is not momentary or temporary; it is for life! That fact alone gives you reason to rejoice and sing.

No matter what you're facing, remember these two words from Psalm 30:5: "joy comes." Take a lesson from the Israelites at Jericho and start shouting before the walls fall. Your joy is around the corner!

NOTES:

PSALM 31
NEW KING JAMES VERSION

¹ In You, O LORD, I put my trust;
Let me never be ashamed;
Deliver me in Your righteousness.
² Bow down Your ear to me,
Deliver me speedily;
Be my rock of refuge,
A fortress of defense to save me.

³ For You are my rock and my fortress;
Therefore, for Your name's sake,
Lead me and guide me.
⁴ Pull me out of the net which they have secretly laid for me,
For You are my strength.
⁵ Into Your hand I commit my spirit;
You have redeemed me, O LORD God of truth.

⁶ I have hated those who regard useless idols;
But I trust in the LORD.
⁷ I will be glad and rejoice in Your mercy,
For You have considered my trouble;
You have known my soul in adversities,
⁸ And have not shut me up into the hand of the enemy;
You have set my feet in a wide place.

⁹ Have mercy on me, O LORD, for I am in trouble;
My eye wastes away with grief,
Yes, my soul and my body!
¹⁰ For my life is spent with grief,
And my years with sighing;
My strength fails because of my iniquity,
And my bones waste away.

*¹¹ I am a reproach among all my enemies,
But especially among my neighbors,
And am repulsive to my acquaintances;
Those who see me outside flee from me.
¹² I am forgotten like a dead man, out of mind;
I am like a broken vessel.
¹³ For I hear the slander of many;
Fear is on every side;
While they take counsel together against me,
They scheme to take away my life.*

*¹⁴ But as for me, I trust in You, O LORD;
I say, "You are my God."
¹⁵ My times are in Your hand;
Deliver me from the hand of my enemies,
And from those who persecute me.
¹⁶ Make Your face shine upon Your servant;
Save me for Your mercies' sake.*

29

THE LAST WORDS OF JESUS
PSALM 31

Have you ever considered the last words Jesus spoke while dying on the cross came from the Psalms of David? Luke 23:46 tells us He spoke the words David penned in Psalm 31:5: "Into Your hand I commit my spirit." Jesus was telling the Father that He completely trusted Him in the face of death. I suppose if Jesus spoke the psalms while dying, it would be a great practice for the living. I would like to encourage you to find a verse that ministers to you and speak it throughout your day. Here are a few of my favorite verses from Psalm 31.

Psalm 31:3 says, "For You are my rock and my fortress; Therefore, for Your name's sake, Lead me and guide me." God is a fortress, impenetrable by the enemy. In the second verse, David described God as "a fortress of defense to save me."

In Psalm 31:7, 8 David declared that God is aware of our adversities and keeps us in a secure place. Sometimes the affairs of life leave us feeling all alone, and we question God's care and presence. But the Bible assures us that He is fully aware of and concerned about every detail of our lives.

Psalm 31:14 says, "But as for me, I trust in You, O Lord; I say, 'You are my God.'" Like David, we need to declare, "God, You are my God." We must make this truth a personal one. He is not an impersonal God. Hebrew 4:15 promises that He sympathizes with our weaknesses. God knows and understands what we are going through. Hebrews 4:15,16 continues, "(Jesus) was in all points tempted as we are, yet without sin. Let us therefore come boldly to the throne of grace, that we may obtain mercy and find grace to help in time of need."

Christianity is the only religion in the world that teaches God came down to the level of man. Every false religion teaches that man has to do something to get to God. (See Philippians 2:5-8.) All we have to do is believe God's Word and act upon it. Jesus did the rest.

PSALM 32
NEW KING JAMES VERSION

¹ Blessed is he whose transgression is forgiven,
Whose sin is covered.
² Blessed is the man to whom the LORD does not impute iniquity,
And in whose spirit there is no deceit.

³ When I kept silent, my bones grew old
Through my groaning all the day long.
⁴ For day and night Your hand was heavy upon me;
My vitality was turned into the drought of summer. Selah
⁵ I acknowledged my sin to You,
And my iniquity I have not hidden.
I said, "I will confess my transgressions to the LORD,"
And You forgave the iniquity of my sin. Selah

⁶ For this cause everyone who is godly shall pray to You
In a time when You may be found;
Surely in a flood of great waters
They shall not come near him.
⁷ You are my hiding place;
You shall preserve me from trouble;
You shall surround me with songs of deliverance. Selah

⁸ I will instruct you and teach you in the way you should go;
I will guide you with My eye.
⁹ Do not be like the horse or like the mule,
Which have no understanding,
Which must be harnessed with bit and bridle,
Else they will not come near you.

¹⁰ Many sorrows shall be to the wicked;
But he who trusts in the LORD, mercy shall surround him.
¹¹ Be glad in the LORD and rejoice, you righteous;
And shout for joy, all you upright in heart!

30

MULES
PSALM 32

When David wrote Psalm 32, he'd had time to reflect upon the mercy of God extended to him after his sin of adultery with Bathsheba. Two of the most powerful verses in the Bible are found in this psalm: "Blessed is he whose transgression is forgiven, Whose sin is covered. Blessed is the man to whom the Lord does not impute (charge his account with) iniquity, And in whose spirit there is no deceit" (verses 1, 2).

Notice one specific key in verse 2: "In whose spirit there is no deceit." Following these verses, David detailed the misery he felt from hiding his sin. The weight of his transgression was about to eat him alive. He wrote in verses 3 and 4: "When I kept silent, my bones grew old through my groaning all the day long. For day and night Your hand was heavy upon me; My vitality was turned into the drought of summer." Refusing to repent takes a great toll on one's life and body. Perhaps that is why David wrote in verse 9: "Do not be like the horse or like the mule, Which have no understanding, Which must be harnessed with bit and bridle, Else they will not come near you." In other words, don't be as stubborn as mules.

Another key is found in verse 4: "For day and night Your hand was heavy upon me." God loved David so much He wouldn't let him go. I am so thankful for God's relentless hold on us. We can never escape His mercy and goodness. At times, His dealings with us may seem harsh, but they are only an expression of His goodness.

If you need God's forgiveness for anything, run to Him. Do not deceive yourself and think you will be all right without Him. David said in verse 2, "Blessed is the man…in whose spirit there is no deceit." The only way to live is to come clean with God.

Now, here is the greatest news in the world – God forgives everything! You need not hold onto your sins or faults through shame. Jesus took your shame and nailed it to the cross. David probably held onto his guilt too long because he was ashamed.

Sin is a serious issue, and God wants us to live free from its burden. The Apostle John said it well in 1 John 2:1: "My little children (meaning believers), these things I write to you, so that you may not sin. And if anyone sins, we have an Advocate with the Father, Jesus Christ the Righteous. And He Himself is the propitiation for our sins, and not for ours only but also for the whole world." God doesn't want us to sin, nor does He want us to hold onto shame when we do sin.Repentance is the required action for sin. Simply run to Jesus; His arms are open.

NOTES:

PSALM 34
NEW KING JAMES VERSION

¹ I will bless the LORD at all times;
His praise shall continually be in my mouth.
² My soul shall make its boast in the LORD;
The humble shall hear of it and be glad.
³ Oh, magnify the LORD with me,
And let us exalt His name together.

⁴ I sought the LORD, and He heard me,
And delivered me from all my fears.
⁵ They looked to Him and were radiant,
And their faces were not ashamed.
⁶ This poor man cried out, and the LORD heard him,
And saved him out of all his troubles.
⁷ The angel of the LORD encamps all around those who fear Him,
And delivers them.

⁸ Oh, taste and see that the LORD is good;
Blessed is the man who trusts in Him!
⁹ Oh, fear the LORD, you His saints!
There is no want to those who fear Him.
¹⁰ The young lions lack and suffer hunger;
But those who seek the LORD shall not lack any good thing.

¹¹ Come, you children, listen to me;
I will teach you the fear of the LORD.
¹² Who is the man who desires life,
And loves many days, that he may see good?
¹³ Keep your tongue from evil,
And your lips from speaking deceit.
¹⁴ Depart from evil and do good;
Seek peace and pursue it.

¹⁵ The eyes of the LORD are on the righteous,
And His ears are open to their cry.

¹⁶ The face of the LORD is against those who do evil,
To cut off the remembrance of them from the earth.

¹⁷ The righteous cry out, and the LORD hears,
And delivers them out of all their troubles.
¹⁸ The LORD is near to those who have a broken heart,
And saves such as have a contrite spirit.

¹⁹ Many are the afflictions of the righteous,
But the LORD delivers him out of them all.
²⁰ He guards all his bones;
Not one of them is broken.
²¹ Evil shall slay the wicked,
And those who hate the righteous shall be condemned.
²² The LORD redeems the soul of His servants,
And none of those who trust in Him shall be condemned.

31

CHANGE YOUR ACT
PSALM 34

David had just pulled off a good act when he wrote Psalm 34. He had fled from Saul to Achish in Gath and feigned madness for fear of losing his life. He must have been a pretty good actor, because everyone was convinced he had lost his mind. I suspect God had given him this brilliant idea.

David's little show took place right after Saul had slaughtered the city of Nob, a city David had just visited. (See Devotion Psalm 52.) David came to Gath looking for refuge, but he quickly realized the people viewed him as a threat and would probably kill him. First Samuel 21:13 records the story: "So he changed his behavior before them, pretended madness in their hands, scratched on the doors of the gate, and let his saliva fall down on his beard." That was a pretty good act! I wonder if the idea came from God. Perhaps God told David to change his act. Obviously, the idea worked!

Maybe some of you today are facing situations where you should change your act. Although that idea has an interesting twist, I do know that from time to time we need to change our act. Now, I'm not suggesting that you act crazy. I'm simply proposing there are times when we are acting one way, but need to change our act and act another way.

In David's case, he was facing some pretty dire circumstances. (See 1 Samuel 21 and 22.) Of course, things are not always as they appear. Perhaps, like David, you are confronting difficult circumstances. God may be suggesting you change how you are looking at them. Are you looking at the problem or at the Answer to the problem?

The entire 34th Psalm is a song David sings to the Lord about the happiness of those who trust in God. David definitely had reason to rejoice. In verse 6, he wrote, "This poor man cried out, and the Lord heard him, And saved him out of all his troubles." David continued in verse 15, "The eyes of the Lord are on the righteous, and His ears are open to their cry."

I am not going to suggest how you should change your act, for my job is to focus on me. Being far from perfect, I know there are things in my own life I can change. For instance, I need to be more conscious of God throughout the day and not just during devotion time. David wisely said, "I will bless the Lord at all times; His praise shall continually be in my mouth." Another way to change your act is to "boast in the Lord" (verse 2). When success comes your way, give God the glory. James 1:17 reminds us that "Every good and every perfect gift is from above and comes down from the Father..."

Today, remember to keep your eyes on the Lord and give him praise for His goodness. As you think upon the faithfulness of God, you might find yourself changing your act.

PSALM 35
NEW KING JAMES VERSION

¹ Plead my cause, O LORD, with those who strive with me;
Fight against those who fight against me.
² Take hold of shield and buckler,
And stand up for my help.
³ Also draw out the spear,
And stop those who pursue me.
Say to my soul,
"I am your salvation."

⁴ Let those be put to shame and brought to dishonor
Who seek after my life;
Let those be turned back and brought to confusion
Who plot my hurt.
⁵ Let them be like chaff before the wind,
And let the angel of the LORD chase them.
⁶ Let their way be dark and slippery,
And let the angel of the LORD pursue them.

32

THE INVISIBLE MAN
PSALM 35

All through his cave years, David experienced attacks from others. But instead of trying to defend himself, he relied on God to take care of him. He wrote in Psalm 35:5: "Let the angel of the Lord chase them." Because angels are invisible, we don't often think about them. David, however, understood their powerful presence and capability. He knew this "invisible man" would "pursue" his enemies (verse 6).

Angels are among the great arsenal of things God can use to defend and protect His people. Although we can't see angels with our physical eyes, they are all around us. Angels have a divine purpose for our benefit. Hebrews 1:14 says this about angels: "Are they not all ministering spirits sent forth to minister for those who will inherit salvation?"

Surprisingly enough, there are more direct references to angels in the New Testament than in the Old Testament. A careful examination will reveal that the New Testament activity of angels usually revolved around the ministry of Jesus and the establishment of His church on the earth. Angels are ministering spirits, or heavenly assistants, who are continually active today in building the Body of Christ, advancing the ministry of Jesus and the building of His church. For example, we find in Matthew 4:11 that, at the conclusion of the temptation of Jesus by Satan in the wilderness, "the devil left Him, and behold, angels came and ministered to Him." Angels are invisibly present in the assemblies of Christians and are appointed by God to minister to believers.

Although angels have appeared to people, we are not to seek visible, physical manifestations of angels. We are to accept, by faith, their existence and their purpose. We are not to worship angels because they are not God. They are on assignment from God. That is why David could confidently say, "Let the angel of the Lord pursue them."

Today, give thanks to God for establishing the ministry of His angels on your behalf. Psalm 91:11 promises "For He shall give His angels charge over you, To keep you in all your ways." Angels are on assignment from God for you!

NOTES:

PSALM 36
NEW KING JAMES VERSION

*¹ An oracle within my heart concerning
the transgression of the wicked:
There is no fear of God before his eyes.
² For he flatters himself in his own eyes,
When he finds out his iniquity and when he hates.
³ The words of his mouth are wickedness and deceit;
He has ceased to be wise and to do good.
⁴ He devises wickedness on his bed;
He sets himself in a way that is not good;
He does not abhor evil.*

*⁵ Your mercy, O LORD, is in the heavens;
Your faithfulness reaches to the clouds.
⁶ Your righteousness is like the great mountains;
Your judgments are a great deep;
O LORD, You preserve man and beast.*

*⁷ How precious is Your lovingkindness, O God!
Therefore the children of men put their trust under the shadow of Your
wings.
⁸ They are abundantly satisfied with the fullness of Your house,
And You give them drink from the river of Your pleasures.
⁹ For with You is the fountain of life;
In Your light we see light.*

*¹⁰ Oh, continue Your lovingkindness to those who know You,
And Your righteousness to the upright in heart.
¹¹ Let not the foot of pride come against me,
And let not the hand of the wicked drive me away.
¹² There the workers of iniquity have fallen;
They have been cast down and are not able to rise.*

33

NO COMPARISON
PSALM 36

This psalm can be divided into two segments. Verses 1-4 describe the wicked, while in stark contrast, verses 5-12 depict the character of the Lord. There is no comparison between the wicked and the Lord. Let's focus today on God's character as described by David.

First, David wrote in verse 5, "Your mercy, O Lord, is in the heavens." He did not say His mercy was in the sky. It's possible for man to get to the sky – it's done every day by airplane and other methods. But man cannot travel to the heavens. The heavens are an unattainable destination. Man has made it to the moon, but that is nothing compared to the heavens of this vast universe. Like the heavens, God's mercy is unattainable unless God makes it so. Thankfully, He has made His mercy available to all.

Mercy is only one of God's many attributes David described in Psalm 36. Verse by verse, David continued to list outstanding qualities of God's character. In verses 5 and 6, he said God's "faithfulness reaches to the clouds" and His "righteousness is like the great mountains." Verse 7 says, "How precious is Your loving kindness, O God!" Verse 8 says that God gives us "drink from the river of His pleasures." In verse 9, David said to the Lord, "For with You is the fountain of life." The list of the amazing attributes of God is endless. When one compares God to the enemy and the wicked, there is no comparison. It is a no-brainer when it comes to choosing whom to serve.

However, we must be mindful of Satan's tactics. Because he is a great deceiver, he always tries to show an upside to the things he tempts us with. I would be foolish to say there is not pleasure in sin. Satan will bait you with the pleasure of sin, but he'll never show you the end result. God is the one who will show you the repercussions of sin. He said in Romans 6:23, "The wages of sin is death." The end result of sin, which Satan always hides, is death.

God gives us the privilege of choosing life. His way is life. Remember David's words from Psalm 36: "With You is the fountain of life." We can choose death (Satan's way) or life (God's way). When we get down to it, there is no comparison. God's way is the best!

NOTES:

PSALM 37
NEW KING JAMES VERSION

¹ Do not fret because of evildoers,
Nor be envious of the workers of iniquity.
² For they shall soon be cut down like the grass,
And wither as the green herb.

³ Trust in the LORD, and do good;
Dwell in the land, and feed on His faithfulness.
⁴ Delight yourself also in the LORD,
And He shall give you the desires of your heart.

⁵ Commit your way to the LORD,
Trust also in Him,
And He shall bring it to pass.
⁶ He shall bring forth your righteousness as the light,
And your justice as the noonday.

⁷ Rest in the LORD, and wait patiently for Him;
Do not fret because of him who prospers in his way,
Because of the man who brings wicked schemes to pass.
⁸ Cease from anger, and forsake wrath;
Do not fret—it only causes harm.

⁹ For evildoers shall be cut off;
But those who wait on the LORD,
They shall inherit the earth.
¹⁰ For yet a little while and the wicked shall be no more;
Indeed, you will look carefully for his place,
But it shall be no more.
¹¹ But the meek shall inherit the earth,
And shall delight themselves in the abundance of peace.

34

ECONOMIC INJUSTICE
PSALM 37

Full of strength and encouragement, Psalm 37 is great for meditation. It is a psalm written to men, rather than to God, and contrasts the lifestyle of the wicked and deceitful with the righteous and forgiven. Emphasizing the secure future of the righteous Jews, this psalm mentions the phrase "dwell in the land" or "inherit the land" eight times. Let's take a look at God's economic justice as described in Psalm 37.

It would be easy to be deceived into believing God is not just, especially when evil people seem to flourish. Scripture is clear we should not "be envious" of them (verses 1 and 7), for their momentary pleasure will quickly pass (verses 2 and 9). It can be very difficult if you are a giving, obedient child of God and are struggling financially. Many times you will see ungodly people flourish because they honor natural laws like hard work, discipline, and common sense. I personally believe the first tenth (Biblical tithe) belongs to the Lord, and He allows us to be stewards (managers) of the other 90%. He owns everything, and we are managers of what He puts in our hands. Just because I honor the Lord with my tithe, I am not entitled to be a poor, undisciplined manager of the other 90%. Imagine the power of combining the tithe with hard work and financial wisdom!

Instead of focusing on seeming economic injustice, we are commanded in Psalm 37:3 to feed on the faithfulness of God. The believer who patiently waits for the timing of God has nothing to fear or be envious about, because God is faithful to His Word. We are to stay faithful to God with His portion and ask Him for wisdom in managing the other 90%.

The world is currently focused on social and economic justice. Headlines are filled with words like "government bailout." The only way government can "bail out" anyone is to borrow or to take from one and give to another. Some people call the latter economic justice. But in God's kingdom, economics follow a different pattern. Because God owns everything, He never needs to borrow. He's never had to take from one to give to another. He has plenty of resources to meet all the needs of those who trust Him.

Trusting God is the key to our economic success. God's people must actively, consciously trust that God's Word is true and that He always acts in accordance with it. Every situation we encounter is an opportunity to choose to trust God rather than our own inclinations. Faith involves an element of risk, but it always yields the richest of dividends. Notice what David said in Psalm 37:5,6: "Commit your way to the Lord, Trust also in Him, And He shall bring it to pass. He shall bring forth your righteousness as the light, And your justice as the noonday."

Recently, a close friend told me that because the economy has recently been very tight, she had allowed fear to control her heart and she had reduced her giving. Notice the reason she cited was fear. (See Psalm 53 devotion.) The Bible tells us that fear involves torment (I John 4:18). My friend realized she should not allow fear to dictate her faith and trust in God.

I encourage you to begin focusing on God as your source instead of looking at the apparent injustice in today's shaky economy. God is not a resource; He is the source! Today, meditate on David's words from Psalm 37:4: "Delight yourself also in the Lord, And He shall give you the desires of your heart."

NOTES:

PSALM 38
NEW KING JAMES VERSION

¹ *O LORD, do not rebuke me in Your wrath,*
Nor chasten me in Your hot displeasure!
² *For Your arrows pierce me deeply,*
And Your hand presses me down.

³ *There is no soundness in my flesh*
Because of Your anger,
Nor any health in my bones
Because of my sin.
⁴ *For my iniquities have gone over my head;*
Like a heavy burden they are too heavy for me.
⁵ *My wounds are foul and festering*
Because of my foolishness.

⁶ *I am troubled, I am bowed down greatly;*
I go mourning all the day long.
⁷ *For my loins are full of inflammation,*
And there is no soundness in my flesh.
⁸ *I am feeble and severely broken;*
I groan because of the turmoil of my heart.

⁹ *Lord, all my desire is before You;*
And my sighing is not hidden from You.
¹⁰ *My heart pants, my strength fails me;*
As for the light of my eyes, it also has gone from me.

¹¹ *My loved ones and my friends stand aloof from my plague,*
And my relatives stand afar off.
¹² *Those also who seek my life lay snares for me;*
Those who seek my hurt speak of destruction,
And plan deception all the day long.

¹³ *But I, like a deaf man, do not hear;*
And I am like a mute who does not open his mouth.

¹⁴ Thus I am like a man who does not hear,
And in whose mouth is no response.

¹⁵ For in You, O LORD, I hope;
You will hear, O Lord my God.
¹⁶ For I said, "Hear me, lest they rejoice over me,
Lest, when my foot slips, they exalt themselves against me."

¹⁷ For I am ready to fall,
And my sorrow is continually before me.
¹⁸ For I will declare my iniquity;
I will be in anguish over my sin.
¹⁹ But my enemies are vigorous, and they are strong;
And those who hate me wrongfully have multiplied.
²⁰ Those also who render evil for good,
They are my adversaries, because I follow what is good.

²¹ Do not forsake me, O LORD;
O my God, be not far from me!
²² Make haste to help me,
O Lord, my salvation!

35

OUCH!
PSALM 38

At times, we all are in need of correction. It is a spiritual fact that no one is perfect. The Apostle Paul, in writing to Titus (a young pastor with the challenging task of setting in order the church at Crete) said, "Rebuke with all authority." Ouch!

Although correction may seem harsh, it is necessary for us to grow. Job 5:17 says, "Behold, happy is the man whom God corrects; Therefore do not despise the chastening of the Almighty." Hebrews 12:5,6 says, "My son, do not despise the chastening of the Lord, Nor be discouraged when you are rebuked by Him; for whom the Lord loves He chastens..." Hebrews 12:11 gives us another good reason for correction: "Now no chastening seems to be joyful for the present, but painful; nevertheless, afterward it yields the peaceable fruit of righteousness to those who have been trained by it." Obviously, correction from the Lord is good for us.

I vividly remember getting corrected as a child. My parents believed in the belt, although it probably wasn't used as much as it was needed. Like any child, I did not like the belt. Despite its stinging affects, I still remember it. I can even remember some things I did that got me the belt. I quickly learned it was not to my benefit to do those things! That is the lesson God wants us to learn. These "chastening" experiences are for our benefit.

David started Psalm 38 by recognizing the Lord's chastening. He simply asked for it not to be administered in wrath and anger. In verses 4 and 18, David talked about his sins. He knew he was guilty but didn't want to face God's wrath.

Thankfully, we don't have to face God's wrath for our sins because Jesus already took care of the sin problem. He provided atonement if we repent or "turn away from" sin. In childhood, if we turned away from the thing that displeased our earthly fathers, we did not receive further chastening from them. It is like that with our Heavenly Father. When we "turn away" from those things that displease Him, we will not receive further chastening.

God's correction is a good thing, not a bad thing. Proverbs 3:12 says, "For whom the Lord loves He corrects, Just as a father the son in whom he delights." Let's welcome the correction of our loving, Heavenly Father.

PSALM 39
NEW KING JAMES VERSION

¹ I said, "I will guard my ways, lest I sin with my tongue;
I will restrain my mouth with a muzzle,
While the wicked are before me."
² I was mute with silence, I held my peace even from good;
And my sorrow was stirred up.
³ My heart was hot within me; while I was musing, the fire burned.
Then I spoke with my tongue:

⁴ "LORD, make me to know my end,
and what is the measure of my days,
That I may know how frail I am.
⁵ Indeed, You have made my days as handbreadths,
And my age is as nothing before You;
Certainly every man at his best state is but vapor. Selah
⁶ Surely every man walks about like a shadow;
Surely they busy themselves in vain; he heaps up riches,
And does not know who will gather them.

⁷ "And now, Lord, what do I wait for? My hope is in You.
⁸ Deliver me from all my transgressions;
Do not make me the reproach of the foolish.
⁹ I was mute, I did not open my mouth, because it was You who did it.
¹⁰ Remove Your plague from me;
I am consumed by the blow of Your hand.
¹¹ When with rebukes You correct man for iniquity,
You make his beauty melt away like a moth;
Surely every man is vapor. Selah

¹² "Hear my prayer, O LORD, and give ear to my cry;
Do not be silent at my tears; for I am a stranger with You,
A sojourner, as all my fathers were.
¹³ Remove Your gaze from me, that I may regain strength,
Before I go away and am no more."

36

BIG TROUBLEMAKER
PSALM 39

Psalm 39:1 is a strong statement: "I said, 'I will guard my ways, Lest I sin with my tongue; I will restrain my mouth with a muzzle, While the wicked are before me.'" When I read this verse, I pictured a dog with a muzzle on it. A muzzle is used to keep animals from biting. As adult humans, we tend to bite more with our tongue than with our teeth. James 3:1-12 reveals the tongue as a big troublemaker. From this passage in Psalms, it's evident David understood the power of the tongue.

Verse two reveals that David possibly bit his tongue, so to speak. He wasn't going to say anything until he could control what he said. That is easier said than done. Personally, I have experienced times I would have been better off biting my tongue instead of saying what I did.

As I meditated this psalm, I was struck by David's control over his tongue. I was equally impressed by the revelation of when and to whom he spoke. As David held his tongue, his heart turned toward God (verse 3). Instead of railing on the people he had issues with, he poured his complaint with them out to God. When he could hold it no longer, David did not pop off his mouth to the enemy, but rather he poured it out to God.

I am not sure what specific circumstances David was facing. Verse 9 indicates he may have been refraining from blaming others. It is so easy to blame someone else instead of being quiet and looking in the mirror first.

One thing is certain - I have less trouble in life when I control my big troublemaker, my tongue. Notice what David said in verse 8: "Deliver me from all my transgressions; Do not make me the reproach of the foolish." Perhaps he knew the pain of opening his mouth too quickly and ending up with the proverbial egg on his face. Let's take a lesson from David and bite our tongues and wait to speak until we can open our mouth to God.

NOTES:

PSALM 40
NEW KING JAMES VERSION

¹ *I waited patiently for the LORD;*
And He inclined to me,
And heard my cry.
² *He also brought me up out of a horrible pit,*
Out of the miry clay,
And set my feet upon a rock,
And established my steps.
³ *He has put a new song in my mouth—*
Praise to our God;
Many will see it and fear,
And will trust in the LORD.

⁴ *Blessed is that man who makes the LORD his trust,*
And does not respect the proud, nor such as turn aside to lies.
⁵ *Many, O LORD my God, are Your wonderful works*
Which You have done;
And Your thoughts toward us
Cannot be recounted to You in order;
If I would declare and speak of them,
They are more than can be numbered.

⁶ *Sacrifice and offering You did not desire;*
My ears You have opened.
Burnt offering and sin offering You did not require.
⁷ *Then I said, "Behold, I come;*
In the scroll of the book it is written of me.
⁸ *I delight to do Your will, O my God,*
And Your law is within my heart."

⁹ *I have proclaimed the good news of righteousness*
In the great assembly;
Indeed, I do not restrain my lips,
O LORD, You Yourself know.

¹⁰ I have not hidden Your righteousness within my heart;
I have declared Your faithfulness and Your salvation;
I have not concealed Your lovingkindness and Your truth
From the great assembly.

¹¹ Do not withhold Your tender mercies from me, O LORD;
Let Your lovingkindness and Your truth continually preserve me.
¹² For innumerable evils have surrounded me;
My iniquities have overtaken me, so that I am not able to look up;
They are more than the hairs of my head;
Therefore my heart fails me.

¹³ Be pleased, O LORD, to deliver me;
O LORD, make haste to help me!
¹⁴ Let them be ashamed and brought to mutual confusion
Who seek to destroy my life;
Let them be driven backward and brought to dishonor
Who wish me evil.
¹⁵ Let them be confounded because of their shame,
Who say to me, "Aha, aha!"

¹⁶ Let all those who seek You rejoice and be glad in You;
Let such as love Your salvation say continually,
"The LORD be magnified!"
¹⁷ But I am poor and needy;
Yet the LORD thinks upon me.
You are my help and my deliverer;
Do not delay, O my God.

37

DEAD SEA MUD
PSALM 40

The writings of David are filled with vivid pictures from Israel, the land in which he lived. While he was running from Saul, David spent time hiding in the cave at Ein Gedi. Today the area is a natural preserve maintained by the state. It sits very near the Dead Sea.

The Dead Sea contains some of the richest minerals in the world. The bottom is an extremely thick mud called Dead Sea mud. Dermatologists extol its power to cleanse and revitalize the skin. If you are not careful, you can get your feet stuck in the mucky, gooey, mineral-rich bottom. Perhaps Dead Sea mud is the source of David's "miry clay" image in verse 2: "He also brought me up out of a horrible pit, Out of the miry clay, And set my feet upon a rock, And established my steps." David was rejoicing that God had redeemed his life from a big, sticky mess. Not only did God bring him out of mud, but He also put a new song in his mouth (verse 3).

Let's take a look at another truth in Psalm 40:8: "I delight to do Your will, O my God, And Your law is within my heart." I have often wondered why David declared, "I delight to do Your will, O my God." Was he having a hard time wanting to do the will of God? Sometimes the will of the flesh and the will of the Spirit have a hard time meshing.

I remember a time in my life when I knew God wanted me to do something, but I was struggling with it. I had been a pastor but knew the Lord was telling us to leave and move to Tulsa. He was leading us back into an itinerant ministry. Although I knew without doubt this was His leading, in my flesh I did not want to travel. Jesus' words in Matthew 26:41 probably best describe my state at that moment in my life: "The spirit indeed is willing, but the flesh is weak." One day, as I read Psalm 40, I realized I should begin to confess, as did David, "I delight to do Your will, O my God." Shortly after I made that verse my confession of faith, the desire for itinerant ministry began to return to my heart. I willed my flesh to get in line with my spirit.

If you are struggling with obedience, I encourage you to declare Psalm 40:8 until your flesh agrees with what the Spirit of God desires. You will be blessed because Psalm 40:4 says, "Blessed is that man who makes the Lord his trust."

PSALM 41
NEW KING JAMES VERSION

¹ Blessed is he who considers the poor;
The LORD will deliver him in time of trouble.
² The LORD will preserve him and keep him alive,
And he will be blessed on the earth;
You will not deliver him to the will of his enemies.
³ The LORD will strengthen him on his bed of illness;
You will sustain him on his sickbed.

⁴ I said, "LORD, be merciful to me;
Heal my soul, for I have sinned against You."
⁵ My enemies speak evil of me:
"When will he die, and his name perish?"
⁶ And if he comes to see me, he speaks lies;
His heart gathers iniquity to itself;
When he goes out, he tells it.

⁷ All who hate me whisper together against me;
Against me they devise my hurt.
⁸ "An evil disease," they say, "clings to him.
And now that he lies down, he will rise up no more."
⁹ Even my own familiar friend in whom I trusted,
Who ate my bread,
Has lifted up his heel against me.

¹⁰ But You, O LORD, be merciful to me, and raise me up,
That I may repay them.
¹¹ By this I know that You are well pleased with me,
Because my enemy does not triumph over me.
¹² As for me, You uphold me in my integrity,
And set me before Your face forever.

¹³ Blessed be the LORD God of Israel
From everlasting to everlasting!
Amen and Amen."

38

OPPORTUNITY IS EVERYWHERE
PSALM 41

Helping the poor is a key theme of Psalm 41. This is something dear to our hearts, as God's assignment for us the past many years has largely involved helping the poor overseas. The dictionary uses the following words to describe *poor*: lacking money, lacking support, wretchedly lacking, unfortunate, lacking in capability. James 1:27 says, "Pure and undefiled religion before God and the Father is this: to visit orphans and widows in their trouble…" Proverbs 21:13 reads, "Whoever shuts his ears to the cry of the poor will also cry himself and not be heard." Obviously, God wants us to care for the poor. (I might point out that nowhere does God tell us in His Word that He wants governments to handle this.) We all should help those who are unfortunate, lacking in support and money, as well as lacking in capability. Unfortunately, some people are simply not capable of helping themselves.

A few years ago, I experienced a paradigm shift. God began to deal with me that we were to help the poor through our ministry efforts. As I embraced His counsel, one morning I felt the Lord impress me with these thoughts, "I said to help the poor, and I did not say just the Christian poor."

Certainly, we are not to neglect our own. However, it is easy to live in the cocoon of our own Christian community and lose our influence in the large world outside of that community. Did not Christ command us to be "salt and light" in this world? (See Matthew 5:13-16.) Perhaps our light referred to in verse 16 is not a sermon preached in word, but in action.

This verse says, "Let your light so shine before men, that they may see your good works and glorify your Father in heaven."

Our actions of compassion can in many cases be the door that opens a person's heart to God. I am told that the great missionary to India, Mark Buntain, stood before a large crowd to preach the Gospel. He heard a man cry out, "Feed our stomachs and then tell us about your Jesus."Maybe it would be easier for people to hear the real message if hunger pangs were not screaming so loudly.

There are many opportunities around us to help those less fortunate. You do not have to cross an ocean to find them. You may not even need to cross the street. Perhaps your next-door neighbor is lacking something you can provide. As you go about your day, look around you, for opportunity is everywhere.

David noted some great reasons for helping the poor in Psalm 41. He wrote in verse 1, "Blessed is he who considers the poor" and then went on to describe what the Lord will do for those who help the underprivileged. Here are the benefits of considering the poor:

- The Lord will deliver him in time of trouble (verse 1).
- The Lord will preserve him and keep him alive (verse 2).
- He will be blessed on the earth (verse 3).
- The Lord will not deliver him to the will of his enemies (verse 3).
- The Lord will strengthen him and sustain (restore) him on his sick bed (verse 3).

Those are some good reasons for helping the poor! Consider the words of David and open your heart and hands to helping those in need. Opportunity is everywhere to be a blessing and to be blessed in return.

NOTES:

PSALM 51
NEW KING JAMES VERSION

—————————⌒—————————

¹ Have mercy upon me, O God,
According to Your lovingkindness;
According to the multitude of Your tender mercies,
Blot out my transgressions.
² Wash me thoroughly from my iniquity,
And cleanse me from my sin.

³ For I acknowledge my transgressions,
And my sin is always before me.
⁴ Against You, You only, have I sinned,
And done this evil in Your sight—
That You may be found just when You speak,
And blameless when You judge.

⁵ Behold, I was brought forth in iniquity,
And in sin my mother conceived me.
⁶ Behold, You desire truth in the inward parts,
And in the hidden part You will make me to know wisdom.

⁷ Purge me with hyssop, and I shall be clean;
Wash me, and I shall be whiter than snow.
⁸ Make me hear joy and gladness,
That the bones You have broken may rejoice.
⁹ Hide Your face from my sins,
And blot out all my iniquities.

¹⁰ Create in me a clean heart, O God,
And renew a steadfast spirit within me.
¹¹ Do not cast me away from Your presence,
And do not take Your Holy Spirit from me.

¹² Restore to me the joy of Your salvation,
And uphold me by Your generous Spirit.
¹³ Then I will teach transgressors Your ways,
And sinners shall be converted to You.

¹⁴ Deliver me from the guilt of bloodshed, O God,
The God of my salvation,
And my tongue shall sing aloud of Your righteousness.
¹⁵ O Lord, open my lips,
And my mouth shall show forth Your praise.
¹⁶ For You do not desire sacrifice, or else I would give it;
You do not delight in burnt offering.
¹⁷ The sacrifices of God are a broken spirit,
A broken and a contrite heart—
These, O God, You will not despise.

¹⁸ Do good in Your good pleasure to Zion;
Build the walls of Jerusalem.
¹⁹ Then You shall be pleased with the sacrifices of righteousness,
With burnt offering and whole burnt offering;
Then they shall offer bulls on Your altar.

39
GET REAL, MAN!
PSALM 51

Psalm 51 was perhaps the hardest of all the psalms for David to pen. In many psalms, David had been betrayed and rejected by men. But here, David had betrayed his God. God sent the prophet Nathan to reveal and confront David's sin. Until this point, David's sins of adultery with Bathsheba and killing her husband Uriah had been hidden from man. But God knew the sin David had committed. Never be fooled - there are no secrets with God.

David had a choice to make. (You can read the story more fully in 2 Samuel 11 and 12.) David could choose to silence Nathan by killing him too, or he could choose to be honest with himself and deal with his sin. In choosing the path of honesty, David made his first step toward restitution with God.

Psalm 51:6 is an important verse not to be overlooked. It reads, "Behold, You desire truth in the inward parts, And in the hidden part you will make me to know wisdom." In other words, get real, man! No one ever confesses their sins and repents until they come to the point of realizing they must. Right relationship with God does not start with walking down an aisle in church. It starts on the inside. If you do not get real on the inside, you will never make the external move toward God. External actions are always the result of inward actions.

David's affair with Bathsheba did not start by their getting together. It started with David's inward thoughts after he saw her bathing on her rooftop (2 Samuel 11:2).One thing that got David in trouble was idle time. Kings were supposed to be at war with their troops at this time.

Second Samuel 11:1 says, "It happened in the spring of the year, at the time when kings go out to battle, that David....remained at Jerusalem." David wasn't where he was supposed to be.

Sometimes we cannot control what comes across our path or our eyes. What happens internally after that is the key. We can turn toward something wrong, or we can choose to turn away from it. Repentance means to "turn away from." When facing tempting situations, we need to get real with ourselves. It's vital we acknowledge what is going on inside and deal with it God's way, because God desires "truth in the inward parts."

When David faced the truth in his inward parts, he realized he had sinned against God. He wrote in Psalm 51:4, "Against You, You only, have I sinned, And done this evil in Your sight." Yes, David had committed sin with Bathsheba and had sinned against Uriah. But he was going to have to stand before the God Who provided atonement for all sin. This realization led him to start Psalm 51 with "Have mercy upon me, O God, According to Your loving kindness; According to the multitude of Your tender mercies."

Man's way is to exact vengeance, but God's way is to shower us with mercy. Gratefully, His mercy endures forever! (See 1 Chronicles 16:34.) So don't be afraid to get real, man!

Psalm 52
New King James Version

¹ Why do you boast in evil, O mighty man?
The goodness of God endures continually.
² Your tongue devises destruction,
Like a sharp razor, working deceitfully.
³ You love evil more than good,
Lying rather than speaking righteousness. Selah
⁴ You love all devouring words,
You deceitful tongue.

⁵ God shall likewise destroy you forever;
He shall take you away, and pluck you out of your dwelling place,
And uproot you from the land of the living. Selah
⁶ The righteous also shall see and fear,
And shall laugh at him, saying,
⁷ "Here is the man who did not make God his strength,
But trusted in the abundance of his riches,
And strengthened himself in his wickedness."

⁸ But I am like a green olive tree in the house of God;
I trust in the mercy of God forever and ever.
⁹ I will praise You forever,
Because You have done it;
And in the presence of Your saints
I will wait on Your name, for it is good.

40

FACEBOOK
PSALM 52

In Psalm 52, David contrasted himself, a righteous man (verses 8,9), with an evil man named Doeg (verses 1-7). What made it so easy for David to make such a stark contrast? Let's take a look at the story behind this psalm.

In fleeing from King Saul, David went to the city of Nob. Since his men were tired and hungry, David convinced the priest, Ahimelech, to give them some of the holy bread from the temple to eat. David had no sword, and so he also asked Ahimelech for a sword. The only one available was Goliath's sword, which David had left there earlier after killing the giant. I'm sure David never dreamed he would need that particular weapon.

Meanwhile, Doeg, an Edomite soldier, witnessed all this. Doeg had been captured by Saul years earlier and had become one of Saul's loyal followers. One day when Saul was ranting in frustration over not finding David, Doeg revealed his encounter in Nob. Saul then went to Nob and told his soldiers to kill all of Nob's priests, because they had assisted David. Sadly, Doeg killed eighty-five innocent priests (1 Samuel 22:18), while Saul's men slaughtered the people of the city. It is interesting to note that one of Ahimelech's sons, Abiathar, escaped the slaughter, and later became priest in David's kingdom.

The highlights of the story surrounding the writing of Psalm 52 help us to see how David could so easily draw the picture between the righteous and the evil man. David was not quick to make these kinds of judgments, yet he had to be very discerning. He had to discern who was for him and who was against him. Scripture records that right after leaving

Nob, David went to Gath for a short time and then to the cave of Adullam. It was there that God brought to him an army of about 400 men (1 Samuel 22:1, 2). Unlike Doeg, they were good men who supported David.

In the course of life, good people and evil people come across our path. We choose whom to associate with. Sometimes, Christian people have the false sense they are to be "friends" with everybody. That is not true. We are to be discerning in our relationships. We need not hang around the Doeg's of life!

As I write this book, the most popular Internet social network is Facebook. I regularly get "friend" requests from people I do not even know. I know it is just a social term, but the word "friend" is not literal. It is just a friendly term used in this instance. Do not be duped into thinking everyone in the world is your "friend."

Today, ask God for discernment in your relationships. Ask Him to show you those righteous people who will help you become the person God designed you to be. Take note of your true friends and keep the Doeg's out of your life.

NOTES:

PSALM 53
NEW KING JAMES VERSION

[1] The fool has said in his heart,
"There is no God."
They are corrupt, and have done abominable iniquity;
There is none who does good.

[2] God looks down from heaven upon the children of men,
To see if there are any who understand, who seek God.
[3] Every one of them has turned aside;
They have together become corrupt;
There is none who does good,
No, not one.

[4] Have the workers of iniquity no knowledge,
Who eat up my people as they eat bread,
And do not call upon God?
[5] There they are in great fear
Where no fear was,
For God has scattered the bones of him who encamps against you;
You have put them to shame,
Because God has despised them.

[6] Oh, that the salvation of Israel would come out of Zion!
When God brings back the captivity of His people,
Let Jacob rejoice and Israel be glad.

41

FEAR? WHAT FEAR?
PSALM 53

In Psalm 53, David addressed the powerful emotion of fear. Fear is healthy when one fears the Lord, as we are commanded to do many times in Scripture. However, fear can be paralyzing and destructive when initiated from a source outside of God.

Psalm 53:5 says, "There they are in great fear Where no fear was, for God has scattered the bones of him who encamps against you." The first phrase in that verse contains a very powerful concept. It says that you are in great fear when there is nothing to fear! Most of what one fears never comes to pass anyway.

Pam and I recently found out that our daughter, Natalie, is going to have her first child. I cannot describe the thrill, by the way. We noticed that early in her pregnancy, Natalie seemed hesitant and concerned about some things. One day, her mom asked her if she was having a battle with fear. She acknowledged that she was. The enemy was whispering to her that the baby was not healthy, that maybe she was not pregnant. About the same time, I noticed this verse of Scripture. I felt it was for Natalie, so I texted it to her.

Later, when Natalie was at her doctor's appointment, the doctor was unable to detect a heartbeat from the baby. Natalie began to cry. While the nurse went to get the ultrasound machine, Natalie's husband, Eric, got Natalie's phone and began to read this Scripture, as she had saved the text message. The nurse returned with the machine. When she turned it on, there the baby was doing somersaults, alive and well.

Remember, "There they are in great fear where no fear was." If you are battling fear today, you need to say, "Fear, what fear?" According to 2 Timothy 1:7, fear is a spirit: "For God has not given us a spirit of fear, but of power and of love and of a sound mind." Resist the spirit of fear and let it have no root in your mind. God has given you a sound mind, which means clear thinking.

Many years ago, our home was burglarized. I was away preaching in Arizona. Pam and our young children came in the dark house on Wednesday evening after church. Drew, about age 12, was the first in the house. He saw the evidence and screamed to Pam and Natalie, "Get out of the house! We have been robbed!" The police later said the robbers probably ran out the front door just as Pam pulled the car into the garage. Anyway, after Drew's warning, my wife and kids ran back to the car. Pam said she was so flustered that she did not know what to do. She backed out and drove directly across the street to our neighbor's driveway. They could have run there much faster, but fear had robbed her momentarily of clear thinking.

If you allow fear to dominate you, your decisions in life will be greatly confused. That is not God's plan. Not only has God given you power over the spirit of fear, but He's also given you a sound mind so that your thinking will be clear.

The last part of Psalm 53:5 says, "You have put them (your enemies) to shame, because God has despised them." God is committed to seeing that you overcome the enemy of fear. He despises what it does to you. Anytime fear tries to dominate you, remember this psalm. You can rise above fear, because God has given you a sound mind.

NOTES:

PSALM 54
NEW KING JAMES VERSION

¹ Save me, O God, by Your name,
And vindicate me by Your strength.
² Hear my prayer, O God;
Give ear to the words of my mouth.
³ For strangers have risen up against me,
And oppressors have sought after my life;
They have not set God before them. Selah

⁴ Behold, God is my helper;
The Lord is with those who uphold my life.
⁵ He will repay my enemies for their evil.
Cut them off in Your truth.

⁶ I will freely sacrifice to You;
I will praise Your name, O LORD, for it is good.
⁷ For He has delivered me out of all trouble;
And my eye has seen its desire upon my enemies.

42

WRONG SIDE OF
THE MOUNTAIN
PSALM 54

When David was hiding from Saul, he was betrayed by the Ziphites. As a young man, David learned how to respond to betrayal. Although there were many people who betrayed him along the course of his life, David's response was always the same. Before we look at his response, let's look at the story that inspired this psalm in 1 Samuel 23:14-29.

First Samuel 23:14 says David "stayed in strongholds in the Wilderness of Ziph." The locals were referred to as Ziphites. Evidently, the men of Ziph did not feel as if David had a chance of being king. It was supposed self-preservation for them to go to the current king, Saul, and tell him where David was hiding so he could come and kill him. David referred to the Ziphites in Psalm 54:3, saying, "Strangers have risen up against me." Although David did not know they were doing this, God did. Nothing that ever comes against God's people catches God by surprise. As He always does, God had a plan.

First, Saul's son Jonathan, who had enough spiritual discernment to know that David was chosen by God to be king, came "to David in the woods and strengthened his hand in God." I would like to know what he said, but he obviously encouraged David. Isn't that just like God? When your back is against the wall, He sends someone or something to encourage you. He will never allow more to come on us than we can bear. Jonathan did what good friends do, and that is to encourage others in the Lord.

Next, David moved to "the plain on the south of Jeshimon" (verse 24). When Saul and his men came, the people of Jeshimon told David so he could escape. It would have been easy for David to focus on the negative (people of Ziph) and overlook the positive (Jonathan and the people of Jeshimon). But David looked for all the good things God was doing to get him through that difficult situation.

Soon, Saul and his men came to the mountain where David was hiding. They were very close, but not close enough! First Samuel 23:26 says, "Then Saul went on one side of the mountain, and David and his men on the other side of the mountain." Saul's men were on the wrong side of the mountain, which allowed David to escape. Even when it seemed too close for comfort, God had made a way of escape.

As David wrote Psalm 54, he showed the proper response to betrayal and injustice. Let's take a look at his response:

- He relied on and called on God's name and strength for vindication (verse 1)
- He prayed, described his situation, and declared the Lord as his helper (verses 2-4)
- He declared the Lord as helper of those who helped him (verse 4)
- He praised God for who He is and thanked Him for past deliverance (verses 4,7)

While maintaining a right heart and attitude, David trusted God to keep his enemies on the wrong side of the mountain.

If you are facing tough times or situations of betrayal, remember God is on your side. Let David's words be your confession today: "I will freely sacrifice to You; I will praise Your name, O Lord, for it is good. For He has delivered me out of all trouble" (verses 6, 7). God will keep your enemies on the other side of the mountain.

NOTES:

PSALM 55
NEW KING JAMES VERSION

¹ Give ear to my prayer, O God,
And do not hide Yourself from my supplication.
² Attend to me, and hear me;
I am restless in my complaint, and moan noisily,
³ Because of the voice of the enemy,
Because of the oppression of the wicked;
For they bring down trouble upon me,
And in wrath they hate me.

⁴ My heart is severely pained within me,
And the terrors of death have fallen upon me.
⁵ Fearfulness and trembling have come upon me,
And horror has overwhelmed me.
⁶ So I said, "Oh, that I had wings like a dove!
I would fly away and be at rest.
⁷ Indeed, I would wander far off,
And remain in the wilderness. Selah
⁸ I would hasten my escape
From the windy storm and tempest."

⁹ Destroy, O Lord, and divide their tongues,
For I have seen violence and strife in the city.
¹⁰ Day and night they go around it on its walls;
Iniquity and trouble are also in the midst of it.
¹¹ Destruction is in its midst;
Oppression and deceit do not depart from its streets.

¹² For it is not an enemy who reproaches me;
Then I could bear it.
Nor is it one who hates me who has exalted himself against me;
Then I could hide from him.
¹³ But it was you, a man my equal,
My companion and my acquaintance.

¹⁴ We took sweet counsel together,
And walked to the house of God in the throng.

¹⁵ Let death seize them;
Let them go down alive into hell,
For wickedness is in their dwellings and among them.

¹⁶ As for me, I will call upon God,
And the LORD shall save me.
¹⁷ Evening and morning and at noon
I will pray, and cry aloud,
And He shall hear my voice.
¹⁸ He has redeemed my soul in peace from the battle that was against
me,
For there were many against me.
¹⁹ God will hear, and afflict them,
Even He who abides from of old. Selah
Because they do not change,
Therefore they do not fear God.

²⁰ He has put forth his hands against those who were at peace with him;
He has broken his covenant.
²¹ The words of his mouth were smoother than butter,
But war was in his heart;
His words were softer than oil,
Yet they were drawn swords.

²² Cast your burden on the LORD,
And He shall sustain you;
He shall never permit the righteous to be moved.

²³ But You, O God, shall bring them down to the pit of destruction;
Bloodthirsty and deceitful men shall not live out half their days;
But I will trust in You.

43

BACKSTABBER
PSALM 55

I love to fish. Fishing with my son has long been one of my greatest joys in life. I now have a son-in-law who enjoys it as well. We have fun together, but you would not want to be in the boat with us. It can be dangerous with three guys casting with 6-foot rods while bass fishing.

Psalm 55:22 says, "Cast your burden on the Lord, And He shall sustain you; He shall never permit the righteous to be moved (shaken)." The word "burden" has a variety of meanings. In the Hebrew language of the Old Testament, there are eight different words that are translated into the one English word, burden. Here, it can literally be translated "sorrow." Let's look at what has brought sorrow to the heart of David.

David described the extreme emotional pain he was experiencing in verses 4-8, stating that if he had wings he would fly away. The pain was severe. Even if David could fly away, he wouldn't be able to escape the internal pain he was feeling.

We can see who brought him such pain in verses 12-14. In verse 12, David said it wasn't an enemy who had done this to him. This was someone David said he went to church with (verse 14)! Although this may surprise some of you, church-going folk are not perfect.

Ironically, the people closest to you have the potential to cause you the most pain. David found that out the hard way. Most Bible historians believe David was talking about Ahithophel who had been David's counselor, a close and trusted confidant, and one of his best friends. Unfortunately, Ahithophel turned into a backstabbing traitor.

When Absalom, David's son, rebelled and attempted to overthrow David and his kingdom, it began to look like his coup was going to be successful. Thinking he could save his hide and his job, Ahithophel switched his loyalty to Absalom. This crushed David, causing extreme sorrow.

Lest you think this was a petty matter, read verses 20 and 21. You will see that David did nothing to Ahithophel. While all the time saying nice things to David's face, Ahithophel turned into a backstabber.

Although unpleasant, backstabbing and betrayal do happen in this world. I pray it does not come your way. If it has or does in the future, take a lesson from David. He shows you how to handle it in one short verse. In the first twenty-one verses of Psalm 55, David poured out his broken heart to God. Realizing he could not hold onto the hurt, he wrote in verse 22: "Cast your sorrow on the Lord..."

The word "cast" in verse 22 means "violently hurl." When I'm fishing with my son and son-in-law, sometimes we drift a little far from where we want to cast our bait. The further away we drift, the more violently we have to hurl. We fling that bait as hard as we can because we must get it to our intended target. The intended target for your sorrows is into the arms of God. Sometimes it requires a lot of effort because it hurts so severely.

If life's pains have caused you to drift – maybe a little resentment and bitterness have crept in – you have to cast (violently hurl) that junk into the arms of God. By all means, you must get rid of it. You cannot control what happened to you, but you can control what it does or does not do to you. If something or someone has broken your heart, simply cast your sorrow upon the Lord. He will sustain you and pick you up. God will never allow you to be moved or shaken. That's His promise.

Psalm 56
New King James Version

¹ *Be merciful to me, O God, for man would swallow me up;*
Fighting all day he oppresses me.
² My enemies would hound me all day,
For there are many who fight against me, O Most High.

³ Whenever I am afraid, I will trust in You.
⁴ In God (I will praise His word),
In God I have put my trust; I will not fear.
What can flesh do to me?

⁵ All day they twist my words;
All their thoughts are against me for evil.
⁶ They gather together,
They hide, they mark my steps,
When they lie in wait for my life.
⁷ Shall they escape by iniquity?
In anger cast down the peoples, O God!

⁸ You number my wanderings;
Put my tears into Your bottle;
Are they not in Your book?
⁹ When I cry out to You,
Then my enemies will turn back;
This I know, because God is for me.
¹⁰ In God (I will praise His word),
In the LORD (I will praise His word),
¹¹ In God I have put my trust;
I will not be afraid.
What can man do to me?

¹² Vows made to You are binding upon me, O God;
I will render praises to You,
¹³ For You have delivered my soul from death.
Have You not kept my feet from falling,
That I may walk before God
In the light of the living?

44

UNFORTUNATELY, IT'S AN OLD SOVIET AIRPLANE
PSALM 56

While writing this chapter, I was sitting with my wife on an old airplane. The man beside us said in broken English, "Unfortunately, it's an old Soviet airplane." We were on a flight from Simferopol, Ukraine bound for Kiev, Ukraine. The airplane was so old that our seat backs were broken. The name painted on the outside of the plane was Marsland. A trip to Mars may not have provided any greater opportunity for fear. Pam, with firm grip on my hand, prayed almost constantly until we were well into the air.

The inspiration for some of these devotions has come from some very different places, like this unique one. After our neighbor on the plane said, "Unfortunately, it's an old Soviet plane," I quickly thought of David's words in Psalm 56:3: "Whenever I am afraid, I will trust in You." David had written this psalm after he was taken captive by the Philistines in Gath. We can imagine the fear that must have tried to overtake David at this time. In the natural, he was unsure what the outcome would be. The only answer to his insecurity was to trust in God.

Our Kiev-bound flight had me thinking about the concept of trust. Why would I have a tough time trusting God if I was willing to get on that airplane? That airplane was filled with people speaking Russian. I can speak some Russian, but Pam was pretty well oblivious to anything that was said. Maybe that was an advantage in this case. I didn't know the pilot – it was possible he could have just graduated from the sixth grade.

I do not know, because I wasn't allowed to look into the cockpit or to review his credentials. Actually, I am not sure there even was a pilot on that plane. Unlike American flights, we never heard from the captain. We heard the voice of a lady over the intercom. Perhaps there was a baboon pushing play on a tape recorder. Did she exist? Of course, I am being facetious here, but our minds can go wild if we allow them. On that plane, I entrusted my life to someone I had never seen. I also entrusted the life of the woman I love more than anyone in the world to this invisible pilot – a very serious thought now that I think about it.

In David's case, the Philistines thought his life was in their hands. They were wrong! A long time before being taken captive, David had decided to entrust his life to God.

If we can live our lives every day exhibiting complete trust in people we do not even know who have the ability to fail us, why can we not put our trust in God? Even when the flight of life looks a little rough, or the flight plan turns out a little different than we thought, let's choose to sit back, relax, and leave the flying to Him. He has never failed and He never will.

NOTES:

PSALM 57
NEW KING JAMES VERSION

1 Be merciful to me, O God, be merciful to me!
For my soul trusts in You;
And in the shadow of Your wings I will make my refuge,
Until these calamities have passed by.

2 I will cry out to God Most High,
To God who performs all things for me.
3 He shall send from heaven and save me;
He reproaches the one who would swallow me up. Selah
God shall send forth His mercy and His truth.

4 My soul is among lions;
I lie among the sons of men
Who are set on fire,
Whose teeth are spears and arrows,
And their tongue a sharp sword.
5 Be exalted, O God, above the heavens;
Let Your glory be above all the earth.

6 They have prepared a net for my steps;
My soul is bowed down;
They have dug a pit before me;
Into the midst of it they themselves have fallen. Selah

7 My heart is steadfast, O God, my heart is steadfast;
I will sing and give praise.
8 Awake, my glory!
Awake, lute and harp!
I will awaken the dawn.

9 I will praise You, O Lord, among the peoples;
I will sing to You among the nations.
10 For Your mercy reaches unto the heavens,
And Your truth unto the clouds.

11 Be exalted, O God, above the heavens;
Let Your glory be above all the earth.

45

CAVE MAN
PSALM 57

I have always enjoyed camping and sitting by a fire at night. Camping can be a fun experience, but it's not so enjoyable when it becomes a forced way of life for an extended period of time. David spent considerable time camping out, but not by choice. He was hiding from Saul in a cave and probably couldn't even light a fire at night for fear Saul's men would find him. He had truly become a cave man.

When David composed Psalm 57, he was hiding from Saul in the Cave of Adullam. History says Gad, the prophet, came to visit him there. It seems God always had a way to send someone to David for his encouragement when he was trapped or alone. (See devotion for Psalm 142 entitled "Cave Visitors".) God knows exactly where we are and what we are going through when no one else does.

Life in a cave would probably be pretty boring, especially back in the days of the cave man. There certainly would be no ESPN. What does a guy do in a cave? If you take the time to read Psalm 57, you will see what a godly cave man did while he was in the cave.

David's first act in the cave was to pray, perhaps even before he set up camp. In verse 1, he called upon the Lord for His mercy, declaring that his trust was solely in the Lord. He declared he would stay under the shadow of God's wings until the calamities passed. Notice David said, "Until these calamities have passed by." The calamities you experience will pass. They will not last forever. David was declaring to the Lord his faith that God would get him out of the cave.

I love the second verse of Psalm 57: "I will cry out to God Most High, To God who performs all things for me." Our performance won't get us out of calamity. Only God, and that which He performs, will get us through. What a relief that is to me! I know my ability won't get the job done, but His will.

Notice David praised and worshipped God in the cave. Anybody can praise God after they get out of the cave, but it's more challenging to praise Him while still in the cave. God is looking for people who will "rejoice in the Lord always" (Philippians 4:4). Not only was David a worshipper, he was not timid about it either. In Psalm 57:8 he said, "I will awaken the dawn." That's some serious cave man worship!

NOTES:

PSALM 58
NEW KING JAMES VERSION

¹ *Do you indeed speak righteousness, you silent ones?*
Do you judge uprightly, you sons of men?
² *No, in heart you work wickedness;*
You weigh out the violence of your hands in the earth.

³ *The wicked are estranged from the womb;*
They go astray as soon as they are born, speaking lies.
⁴ *Their poison is like the poison of a serpent;*
They are like the deaf cobra that stops its ear,
⁵ *Which will not heed the voice of charmers,*
Charming ever so skillfully.

⁶ *Break their teeth in their mouth, O God!*
Break out the fangs of the young lions, O LORD!
⁷ *Let them flow away as waters which run continually;*
When he bends his bow,
Let his arrows be as if cut in pieces.
⁸ *Let them be like a snail which melts away as it goes,*
Like a stillborn child of a woman, that they may not see the sun.

⁹ *Before your pots can feel the burning thorns,*
He shall take them away as with a whirlwind,
As in His living and burning wrath.
¹⁰ *The righteous shall rejoice when he sees the vengeance;*
He shall wash his feet in the blood of the wicked,
¹¹ *So that men will say,*
"Surely there is a reward for the righteous;
Surely He is God who judges in the earth."

46

DEAF COBRA
PSALM 58

I have always liked sports. Both of our children are athletic, and I loved to watch them play when they were growing up. Not wanting to miss any of their high school games, I would even schedule my travel around their sporting events. I like just about any sport except one – ultimate fighting.

One night while watching television, I came across the ultimate fighting championship. After a few minutes of watching a man get beaten up, I had experienced enough. In this "sport" the two contestants are confined in a chain link cage and almost anything goes. It was gruesome.

By reading Psalm 58:1-5, it seems David was experiencing such a fight. The eventual outcome of that fight was already decided before it even happened. David's enemies did not have to suffer defeat if they would have only listened to the voice of the Lord. Verses 4 and 5 tell us they turned a deaf ear to God's efforts to draw them to Him. David likened them to a "deaf cobra that stops its ears." David went on to say in the next verse that they "will not heed the voice of charmers, charming ever so skillfully." From what I understand, a cobra charmer's goal is to stop the cobra from striking. In other words, his goal is to change the cobra's mind.

Perhaps the greatest power God entrusted to humanity is the power of choice. Unfortunately, sometimes we make the wrong choices. In doing so, we are fighting against God's goodness and mercy. We have the power to choose to change our mind. We can make the right choices in lieu of bad choices, but the choice is up to us.

The ultimate fight is really not against external forces, as David referred to in Psalm 58. The ultimate fight actually is within us. The Apostle Paul talked about it in Romans 7:18-25. To paraphrase, he said, "The evil I don't want to do, sometimes I do. The good I want to do, sometimes I don't do." Paul went to say that the only way to win this ultimate fight is to surrender to Jesus Christ.

Maybe there is something you're struggling with in your heart. While your inclination may be to do a certain thing, the Lord may be pulling you toward that which is right, just like the cobra charmer. The choice belongs to you. The Apostle Paul came to this conclusion in Romans 7:24,25: "O wretched man that I am! Who will deliver me from this body of death? I thank God – through Jesus Christ our Lord!" May we be unlike the deaf cobra and keep our ears open to the Lord.

NOTES:

PSALM 59
NEW KING JAMES VERSION

¹ Deliver me from my enemies, O my God;
Defend me from those who rise up against me.
² Deliver me from the workers of iniquity,
And save me from bloodthirsty men.

³ For look, they lie in wait for my life;
The mighty gather against me,
Not for my transgression nor for my sin, O LORD.
⁴ They run and prepare themselves through no fault of mine.

Awake to help me, and behold!
⁵ You therefore, O LORD God of hosts, the God of Israel,
Awake to punish all the nations;
Do not be merciful to any wicked transgressors. Selah

⁶ At evening they return,
They growl like a dog,
And go all around the city.
⁷ Indeed, they belch with their mouth;
Swords are in their lips;
For they say, "Who hears?"

⁸ But You, O LORD, shall laugh at them;
You shall have all the nations in derision.
⁹ I will wait for You, O You his Strength;
For God is my defense.
¹⁰ My God of mercy shall come to meet me;
God shall let me see my desire on my enemies.

¹¹ Do not slay them, lest my people forget;
Scatter them by Your power,
And bring them down,
O Lord our shield.

¹² For the sin of their mouth and the words of their lips,
Let them even be taken in their pride,
And for the cursing and lying which they speak.

¹³ Consume them in wrath, consume them,
That they may not be;
And let them know that God rules in Jacob
To the ends of the earth. Selah

¹⁴ And at evening they return,
They growl like a dog,
And go all around the city.
¹⁵ They wander up and down for food,
And howl if they are not satisfied.

¹⁶ But I will sing of Your power;
Yes, I will sing aloud of Your mercy in the morning;
For You have been my defense
And refuge in the day of my trouble.
¹⁷ To You, O my Strength, I will sing praises;
For God is my defense,
My God of mercy.

47

EYE OF THE STORM
PSALM 59

The background of this psalm comes from 1 Samuel 18 and 19. David's wife Michal (who happened to be Saul's daughter) had helped David escape from Saul's deathly pursuit. At the writing of Psalm 59, David had just fled from the king. Saul's assassins had tracked him down and were surrounding the house where David was hiding. Although he was surrounded by danger, David remained perfectly calm.

I have lived most of my life in what is commonly called "tornado territory" in northeastern Oklahoma. Tornados can be devastating. Although these storms are extremely impressive in power, they possess a place that is completely calm, called the eye of the storm.

When my wife Pam was a small child, a tornado hit her town of Elk City, Oklahoma. The tornado tore off the front porch and put a crack in her bedroom wall. Surprisingly, she slept right through it! As a child, she was unconcerned about the approaching tornado. Childlike faith helps us sleep through the storm because we cannot do anything about it anyway. Calmness amidst calamity can only come from the Lord. If we develop a childlike trust in God, we can sleep peacefully while He handles the storms.

As mentioned earlier, David was surrounded by Saul and his men. The storm was all around him, but he evidently found peace in the eye of the storm. In Psalm 59:9,10, David said, "…I will wait for You…For God is my defense. My God of mercy shall come to meet me…"

Saul was David's enemy because he chose to be. David could not change it, because Saul was really opposing God, not David. Scripture shows us that Saul tended to often follow his own agenda and not God's. This was very unwise considering God had given him the kingdom in the first place.

Doesn't that sound a lot like Satan and his work? God gave him a prominent place in Heaven, but Satan rebelled against God because he wanted his own way. God took his place from him and cast him from Heaven (Isaiah 14:12-14). Ever since that time, he has been opposing God. The problems that come the way of mankind are the result of Satan's work, not God's. One only needs to read the description of the Garden of Eden in Genesis to understand what God desires for His people. For ages, Satan has tried to take that away from the people of God.

David remained in the eye of the storm through his habit of praising God for past interventions on his behalf (verse 16). God is remarkably present with those who worship Him as He asks. Satan opposes God and everything and everyone that represents Him. Remember that Satan is against you, but God is for you. Satan creates the storm, but God provides the eye of the storm.When you're going through a storm, take time to worship the Lord. As you enter the eye of the storm, everything will be all right.

PSALM 60
NEW KING JAMES VERSION

¹ O God, You have cast us off;
You have broken us down;
You have been displeased;
Oh, restore us again!
² You have made the earth tremble;
You have broken it;
Heal its breaches, for it is shaking.
³ You have shown Your people hard things;
You have made us drink the wine of confusion.

⁴ You have given a banner to those who fear You,
That it may be displayed because of the truth. Selah
⁵ That Your beloved may be delivered,
Save with Your right hand, and hear me.

⁶ God has spoken in His holiness:
"I will rejoice;
I will divide Shechem
And measure out the Valley of Succoth.
⁷ Gilead is Mine, and Manasseh is Mine;
Ephraim also is the helmet for My head;
Judah is My lawgiver.
⁸ Moab is My washpot;
Over Edom I will cast My shoe;
Philistia, shout in triumph because of Me."

⁹ Who will bring me to the strong city?
Who will lead me to Edom?
¹⁰ Is it not You, O God, who cast us off?
And You, O God, who did not go out with our armies?
¹¹ Give us help from trouble,
For the help of man is useless.
¹² Through God we will do valiantly,
For it is He who shall tread down our enemies.

48

GOD'S WILL IS GOD'S BILL
PSALM 60

David penned this psalm in the wake of the disorder following Saul's removal of king. David was soon to be crowned king, and Israel was ready for his leadership. Little did the people realize that on the inside, David was crying out to God, "Who will bring me to the strong city? Who will lead me to Edom?" (verse 9). In other words, David was not going to lead the people unless God led the way.

In the midst of uncertainty, it is important to seek direction from the Lord. Safety and success are determined by relying on His guidance. Romans 8:14 says, "For as many as are led by the Spirit of God, these are the sons of God." It is dangerous to rely strictly on our own wisdom, ability, or strength. There will always be obstacles bigger than we can handle by ourselves.

It almost seems as if David bit off more than he could chew. But David didn't choose to put himself in this place; it was God's choice. David had the monumental task of uniting a divided kingdom. It wasn't an easy job, but God was up to the challenge.

When and where God guides, He provides. It's that simple. The place God leads us to may not always be easy, but it will always have His provision. Pam and I developed a simple motto when God called us to move our family to Ukraine. Our motto was "God's will is God's bill." That same, simple motto has stayed with us through many major steps through which God has lead us.

While you're reading this, you may have a monumental task in front of you. From your current vantage point, you may not know how it will come to pass. I have been there often, yet, all the while experiencing a deep, inner peace. The peace was the result of confidence this was God's will even though I did not know how it would come to pass.

In Psalm 60:9, David asked, "Who will lead me to the strong city?" He was wondering who was going to lead the people against the enemy. The children of Israel were probably looking to him and not God. After all, David was a mighty conqueror, having killed Goliath and many others. Of course, David knew he would have slain no giants without the Lord.

Perhaps like David, you're facing a giant even though you're in the right place God has chosen for you. God has not changed since the days of David. He is "the same, yesterday, today, and forever" (Hebrews 13:8). Remember God's will is God's bill. He is up to the challenge of leading you through to victory!

NOTES:

PSALM 61
NEW KING JAMES VERSION

¹ Hear my cry, O God;
Attend to my prayer.
² From the end of the earth I will cry to You,
When my heart is overwhelmed;
Lead me to the rock that is higher than I.

³ For You have been a shelter for me,
A strong tower from the enemy.
⁴ I will abide in Your tabernacle forever;
I will trust in the shelter of Your wings. Selah

⁵ For You, O God, have heard my vows;
You have given me the heritage of those who fear Your name.
⁶ You will prolong the king's life,
His years as many generations.
⁷ He shall abide before God forever.
Oh, prepare mercy and truth, which may preserve him!

⁸ So I will sing praise to Your name forever,
That I may daily perform my vows.

49

UNDER THE BIG TENT
PSALM 61

Do you remember attending circuses as a child? The ringmaster would always announce in a big, booming voice, "Tonight, under the big tent...." Life can sometimes seem like a circus with clowns, roaring lions, and unbelievable happenings. Despite all the craziness, there is a tent of shelter that covers you.

In Psalm 61, David used four picturesque metaphors to represent God as a shelter: a high rock (verse 2), a fortified tower (verse 3), a pitched tent (verse 4), and a mother hen with outstretched wings (verse 4). Let's consider the tent.

Verse 4 says, "I will abide in Your tabernacle forever." Under the command of God (Exodus 26), the Israelites erected a large tent called the tabernacle. It was here that people came to worship, bringing their sacrifices for the priests to offer unto the Lord. The most inner sanctuary, referred to as the Holy of Holies, contained the Ark of the Covenant and was the dwelling place of the presence of God.

The tent of God's protective presence and abiding peace is gigantic. When our daughter, Natalie, was nine years old, she had a horrific experience. I was hundreds of miles away from Tulsa, where we lived at the time, ministering at a church service. Pam said Natalie came in on this beautiful spring day and asked if she could roller blade around the block one time. Generally, Pam would have her older brother, Drew, go with her but he was at baseball practice. She gave her permission to go one time around the block.

Natalie was on the backside of the block when she noticed a huge car coming slowly behind her. She began to skate as fast as possible, and in her words, "Pray as hard as she could pray." The driver, a man, pulled right beside her, said something vulgar, and exposed himself. Natalie did what all parents teach their children to do. She turned and ran – on roller blades, mind you – through the nearest yard, jumped up on the porch, and screamed at the top of her lungs.

The neighbor residing there heard the scream and opened the front door to find Natalie screaming and the pervert in the car taking off. Alarmed, the neighbor grabbed her and brought her inside. After he brought her home, the police were called and took a detailed report. Before leaving, they warned my wife this was probably the work of a child molester casing a neighborhood. Sadly, about one week later, a man who exactly fit Natalie's description molested a young girl about one mile from our home.

Before I wrote this, I realized this story might cause alarm. However, remember, we are under the big tent. God's presence is no longer confined to the tabernacle; we are His tabernacle. Natalie is his tabernacle. Her Daddy, who would fight tigers to protect her, was nowhere near, but the Great Protector was always by her side.

Today, invoke the power of God's presence to be with you and your family. I make a habit of this. The day this story happened, I quite possibly had done so even though many miles away from home. In God's Kingdom there is no realm of separation, for we live moment by moment under the big tent.

NOTES:

Psalm 62
New King James Version

¹ Truly my soul silently waits for God;
From Him comes my salvation.
² He only is my rock and my salvation;
He is my defense; I shall not be greatly moved.

³ How long will you attack a man?
You shall be slain, all of you,
Like a leaning wall and a tottering fence.
⁴ They only consult to cast him down from his high position;
They delight in lies;
They bless with their mouth, but they curse inwardly. Selah

⁵ My soul, wait silently for God alone,
For my expectation is from Him.
⁶ He only is my rock and my salvation;
He is my defense; I shall not be moved.
⁷ In God is my salvation and my glory;
The rock of my strength, and my refuge, is in God.

⁸ Trust in Him at all times, you people;
Pour out your heart before Him; God is a refuge for us. Selah

⁹ Surely men of low degree are a vapor,
Men of high degree are a lie;
If they are weighed on the scales,
They are altogether lighter than vapor.
¹⁰ Do not trust in oppression,
Nor vainly hope in robbery;
If riches increase, do not set your heart on them.

¹¹ God has spoken once,
Twice I have heard this:
That power belongs to God.
¹² Also to You, O Lord, belongs mercy;
For You render to each one according to his work.

50

TALK TO YOURSELF
PSALM 62

We find David talking to himself in Psalm 62. In verses 5-7, he said, "My soul, wait silently for God alone, For my expectation is from Him. He only is my rock and my salvation; He is my defense. I shall not be moved. In God is my salvation and my glory; the rock of my strength, And my refuge, is in God." The attack on David must have been pretty heavy, and perhaps he was talking to himself to calm down. Verses 2 and 6 show us that he realized his only hope was in God.

Talking to oneself is a Biblical concept. The Apostle Paul put it this way in Ephesians 5:19 (KJV): "Speaking to yourselves in psalms, hymns, and spirit songs, singing and making melody in your heart to the Lord."

There have been times I've talked to myself, speaking God's Word to myself for reassurance. That is basically what David was doing in verse 5 when he wrote, "My soul, wait silently for God…" He was talking to his own soul – his mind, will, and emotions. David told his soul to "wait silently." Now that would be one tall order, especially after people were talking about him behind his back (verse 4).

When people talk about you behind your back, the natural reaction is to do anything but "wait silently." You can't control what people say about you, but you can control your reaction. Notice in verse six David referred to God as his defense. The Lord will defend you better than you can defend yourself. Certainly, there are times you should speak up for yourself. I do believe, however, we too often escalate matters by not waiting silently.

There are two simple principles I hope you glean from this devotional today. First, talk to yourself. Make it a regular practice to speak God's Word to yourself concerning any situation confronting you. Instead of saying what someone else says, say what God says. For example, if you are currently fighting an illness, talk to yourself by saying, "By His stripes we are healed" (Isaiah 53:5). Secondly, "wait silently for God." As you put your trust in Him, you will be able to say as David did, "He only is my rock and salvation; He is my defense; I shall not be moved."

NOTES:

PSALM 63
NEW KING JAMES VERSION

¹ O God, You are my God;
Early will I seek You;
My soul thirsts for You;
My flesh longs for You
In a dry and thirsty land
Where there is no water.
² So I have looked for You in the sanctuary,
To see Your power and Your glory.

³ Because Your lovingkindness is better than life,
My lips shall praise You.
⁴ Thus I will bless You while I live;
I will lift up my hands in Your name.
⁵ My soul shall be satisfied as with marrow and fatness,
And my mouth shall praise You with joyful lips.

⁶ When I remember You on my bed,
I meditate on You in the night watches.
⁷ Because You have been my help,
Therefore in the shadow of Your wings I will rejoice.
⁸ My soul follows close behind You;
Your right hand upholds me.

⁹ But those who seek my life, to destroy it,
Shall go into the lower parts of the earth.
¹⁰ They shall fall by the sword;
They shall be a portion for jackals.

¹¹ But the king shall rejoice in God;
Everyone who swears by Him shall glory;
But the mouth of those who speak lies shall be stopped.

51
KEEP THE MOTOR RUNNING
PSALM 63

Hunger and thirst are great motivators. One day this summer, I went for a walk outside in ninety-degree heat. Of course, I was drenched with perspiration. At the end of the walk, my mind was on one thing – cold water. In fact, I stopped and bought a bottle before returning to the hotel where I was staying. The heat motivated me to get some water quickly!

The words "motor" and "motivation" have the same root. A motor gives thrust or push. Your car has value because of the motor. You could have a Bentley in the garage, but if it has no motor, a 1979 Volkswagen is better if you want to go somewhere. The motor, or motor-vation, is the key. Today, let me ask you this question: What gets your motor running?

I'm intrigued watching people to see what tends to motivate them toward God. I recall during the Persian Gulf War, churches were full everywhere I went. I assume the tense battle in the Middle East had people thinking of end time events. Sadly, I noticed, soon after the hostilities subsided, the church attendance of many people subsided as well. What was the motivation?

A friend of mine recently admitted he lived for years with the attitude of accepting Christ as a "fire insurance policy." He said, "I simply did not want to go to hell." I found this an interesting comment. Sadly, such a motivation leaves one far short of enjoying the life God intends us to live.

In Psalm 63, David was motivated to pursue God. He said in verse 1, "My soul thirsts for You; My flesh longs for You in a dry and thirsty land." His thirst for God motivated him. All through David's life, whenever he was faced with a problem, he turned towards the Lord. He lived a life in relationship with God.

I encourage you to get motivated toward God. By that I mean move toward God. If you are taking time to read this devotional, you are already making a step towards God. Your motor is already propelling you toward Him. Keep the motor running and pursue Him daily, just as David did. As your motor propels you toward God, you can declare, "Because Your loving kindness is better than life, My lips shall praise You...My soul shall be satisfied as with marrow and fatness, And my mouth shall praise You with joyful lips."

NOTES:

PSALM 64
NEW KING JAMES VERSION

¹ Hear my voice, O God, in my meditation;
Preserve my life from fear of the enemy.
² Hide me from the secret plots of the wicked,
From the rebellion of the workers of iniquity,
³ Who sharpen their tongue like a sword,
And bend their bows to shoot their arrows—bitter words,
⁴ That they may shoot in secret at the blameless;
Suddenly they shoot at him and do not fear.

⁵ They encourage themselves in an evil matter;
They talk of laying snares secretly;
They say, "Who will see them?"
⁶ They devise iniquities:
"We have perfected a shrewd scheme."
Both the inward thought and the heart of man are deep.

⁷ But God shall shoot at them with an arrow;
Suddenly they shall be wounded.
⁸ So He will make them stumble over their own tongue;
All who see them shall flee away.
⁹ All men shall fear,
And shall declare the work of God;
For they shall wisely consider His doing.

¹⁰ The righteous shall be glad in the LORD, and trust in Him.
And all the upright in heart shall glory.

52

CAT AND MOUSE GAME
PSALM 64

I have always found the world of espionage intriguing. At the age of 18, I was contemplating a career path like most 18-year-olds. My greatest interest was in the area of criminal justice, until I felt God place His call on my life for ministry. I have never once regretted responding to that call, although I never lost my sense of intrigue with the realm of espionage.

Unlocking difficult cases would be enjoyable. I love those "whodunit" movies. Of course, watching a spy movie is totally different than making a living as a professional detective. The job of a secret agent is what really gets my attention.

It is unknown how much was expended on secret agents during the Cold War, with the USA and the USSR constantly trying to uncover the secret plots of the other. It is a matter of opinion as to which nation was better at that cat and mouse game.

In Psalm 64:2, David prayed, "Hide me from the secret plots of the wicked." He knew his enemies were plotting against him, but he didn't know what they were plotting. David refused to play the cat and mouse game with them; he simply relied on God to expose their plots. We live much the same way today. The enemy plots against God's people, but we are not always aware of his plots.

About 1,000 years after David penned this, we find that Jesus taught His disciples to pray much the same way. He worded it a little differently, putting it like this: "Our Father in heaven, Hallowed be Your name. Your kingdom come, Your will be done On earth as it is in heaven...

And do not lead us into temptation, But deliver us from the evil one" (Matthew 6:10,13). This passage is commonly called the Lord's Prayer, but it is actually the Lord teaching us how to pray every day. Our daily prayer should be that the path the Lord leads us in would bypass temptation and every secret plot the enemy has to do us harm.

In the world of espionage, the spy is trained to find out every move the enemy is planning to gain an advantage over the enemy and to prevent surprise attacks. In God's kingdom, spies are not needed. He already knows everything! You can rely on Him to reveal to you what you need to know. I'm convinced He also often intervenes in our behalf without our even knowing there was a danger. Ask God today for His Holy Spirit to show you things to come and to lead your path around every secret plot of the enemy.

NOTES:

PSALM 65
NEW KING JAMES VERSION

¹ Praise is awaiting You, O God, in Zion;
And to You the vow shall be performed.
² O You who hear prayer, to You all flesh will come.
³ Iniquities prevail against me; As for our transgressions,
You will provide atonement for them.

⁴ Blessed is the man You choose, and cause to approach You,
That he may dwell in Your courts.
We shall be satisfied with
the goodness of Your house, of Your holy temple.

⁵ By awesome deeds in righteousness You will answer us,
O God of our salvation,
You who are the confidence of all the ends of the earth,
And of the far-off seas;
⁶ Who established the mountains by His strength,
Being clothed with power;
⁷ You who still the noise of the seas,
The noise of their waves, and the tumult of the peoples.
⁸ They also who dwell in the farthest parts are afraid of Your signs;
You make the outgoings of the morning and evening rejoice.

⁹ You visit the earth and water it, You greatly enrich it;
The river of God is full of water; You provide their grain,
For so You have prepared it.
¹⁰ You water its ridges abundantly, You settle its furrows;
You make it soft with showers, You bless its growth.

¹¹ You crown the year with Your goodness,
And Your paths drip with abundance.
¹² They drop on the pastures of the wilderness,
And the little hills rejoice on every side.
¹³ The pastures are clothed with flocks;
The valleys also are covered with grain;
They shout for joy, they also sing.

53

AWESOME CHEESEBURGER
PSALM 65

A few years ago, I passed a little restaurant in a small town that had a sign declaring *Home of the World's Most Awesome Cheeseburger*. Although I love cheeseburgers and have eaten them all over the world, I have yet to eat one that is awesome. Many of the ones I've tasted have been great, but none of them literally inspired awe, which is what the word awesome means. In fact, I've experienced very few things that were truly awe-inspiring.

In recent years, the word "awesome" has been thrown around so freely that its true meaning has been diluted. David did not write "awesome" in every other sentence. When he used that word, it was reserved for describing God, not cheeseburgers! (See Psalm 68:35.)

A sunset on the Pacific Ocean can be awe-inspiring. A snow-capped Pikes Peak is awe-inspiring. A full moon with a clear sky filled with millions of stars is awe-inspiring. I could continue, but my point is that anything created by God is awe-inspiring. Nothing man-made makes the grade for me.

In Psalm 65, we read about the awesomeness of God. Not only does God hear us when we pray, but He answers us by "awesome deeds in righteousness" (verse 2 and 5). Wow! He must really care about us.

David spent most of this psalm describing the awesome deeds of God. As you read Psalm 65 today, think about God's awesome deeds that you have witnessed. One of my favorite awesome things God has done is found in Psalm 65:3: "As for our transgressions, You will provide atonement for them." Of all the awe-inspiring acts God has ever performed, this stands high above the rest. Nothing is as awe-inspiring as the fact that God took all my sins, of which there were many, and completely expunged my record of all guilt.

Science tells us east never meets west like north meets south. Unlike the north and south, there are no poles for east and west, because the two never meet. You could walk east a million years and never reach west. The psalmist had that figured out long before science ever did! He wrote in Psalm 103:12, "As far as east is from west, So far has He removed our transgressions from us." Now that is awe-inspiring!

As you pray, do so with confidence. God hears and answers. Most of this psalm describes the awesome creation of God. If the ocean has confidence in the boundaries God has set for it, how much more should we, His children, rest in confidence in what He chooses for us? God is awesome and He always has your best interests at heart!

NOTES:

PSALM 68
NEW KING JAMES VERSION

¹ Let God arise,
Let His enemies be scattered;
Let those also who hate Him flee before Him.
² As smoke is driven away,
So drive them away;
As wax melts before the fire,
So let the wicked perish at the presence of God.
³ But let the righteous be glad;
Let them rejoice before God;
Yes, let them rejoice exceedingly.

⁴ Sing to God, sing praises to His name;
Extol Him who rides on the clouds,
By His name YAH,
And rejoice before Him.

⁵ A father of the fatherless, a defender of widows,
Is God in His holy habitation.
⁶ God sets the solitary in families;
He brings out those who are bound into prosperity;
But the rebellious dwell in a dry land.

⁷ O God, when You went out before Your people,
When You marched through the wilderness, Selah
⁸ The earth shook;
The heavens also dropped rain at the presence of God;
Sinai itself was moved at the presence of God, the God of Israel.
⁹ You, O God, sent a plentiful rain,
Whereby You confirmed Your inheritance,
When it was weary.
¹⁰ Your congregation dwelt in it;
You, O God, provided from Your goodness for the poor.

54

PURE RELIGION
PSALM 68

God places great emphasis upon the family. He established a family before He established a church. From the time of the Garden of Eden, family has been important.

This week Pam and I heard something heartbreaking in Kahovka, Ukraine where our ministry has the privilege of sponsoring an orphanage. We call it House of Joy. There is a very sweet teenage girl in House of Joy, named Luda. As we talked, she recounted how she stood in a courtroom where a judge asked her father, "Do you want to maintain custody of Luda or send her to an orphanage?" He replied, "Send her to an orphanage." Can you imagine the stabbing pain of such rejection?

The good news for Luda and others like her is recorded in Psalm 68:5,6: "A father of the fatherless, a defender of widows, is God in His holy habitation. God sets the solitary in families; He brings out those who are bound into prosperity…" God takes care of the fatherless and widows. His Word describes pure religion for us: "Pure and undefiled religion before God and the Father is this: to visit orphans and widows in their trouble…" (James 1:27).

Not everyone has the same opportunity in regard to family. Due to various circumstances, the world is filled with people who are either alone or feel alone. May I encourage you to minister in some way to the "solitary" – whether an orphan, a widow, or someone alone. God said He "sets the solitary in families." It is our responsibility to care one for another.

The orphaned children at House of Joy are like family to us. We go out of our way to see that their needs are met, because that is what families do. I encourage you to be family to someone who may not have family or may not have family nearby. Go out of your way to fill a void in their life. Rejected and lonely people are all around us. Although we may not know the pain some people are experiencing, God knows all their pain. God knows your pain, too. If you are "solitary," know that God made a promise to you personally when He promised to "set the solitary in families." He will not leave you alone.

Family may not be blood relatives. If you feel alone, your church can be family to you. Don't allow "aloneness" to swallow you. If you are lonely, before someone comes to you, go to someone else who is lonely. God's family is your family!

NOTES:

PSALM 69
NEW KING JAMES VERSION

¹ Save me, O God!
For the waters have come up to my neck.
² I sink in deep mire,
Where there is no standing;
I have come into deep waters,
Where the floods overflow me.
³ I am weary with my crying;
My throat is dry;
My eyes fail while I wait for my God.

⁴ Those who hate me without a cause
Are more than the hairs of my head;
They are mighty who would destroy me,
Being my enemies wrongfully;
Though I have stolen nothing,
I still must restore it.

⁵ O God, You know my foolishness;
And my sins are not hidden from You.
⁶ Let not those who wait for You,
O Lord GOD of hosts, be ashamed because of me;
Let not those who seek You be confounded
because of me, O God of Israel.

55

SQUEAKY WHEEL
GETS THE GREASE
PSALM 69

David provided a graphic picture of his predicament in Psalm 69:1, 2: "Save me, O God! For the waters have come up to my neck. I sink in deep mire, Where there is no standing; I have come into deep waters Where the floods overflow me." He was neck deep in junk.

As you read this psalm, you will see David was overwhelmed even though he had done nothing wrong. Everyone was against him. He was estranged from his brothers (verse 8). The judges of the land were against him (verse 12). Even the drunkards were singing about him (verse 12). How much worse could it have been? There is only one thing to do in such a time – cry out to God. Sometimes the best prayer is simply, "Help!" In Psalm 69, David was placing an urgent plea for help.

There are times we can get so weary that we lose our sense of urgency. Sometimes the obstacle looks so great that our enemy prevails by convincing us there is no hope. But don't fall for the enemy's traps, because Jesus called him a liar! (See John 8:44.)

Examine your life for a moment. Are there things that you at one time prayed urgently for, but today the urgency has gone, maybe because you did not see the answer as quickly as you would have liked? Perhaps you had a glaring need, and once it lost its glare, you put it on the back burner of your prayers. Possibly it is something that intermittently comes to your attention even though the need is very real. It can be like the saying "the squeaky wheel gets the grease," which simply means the thing that is yelling at you the loudest is what you pay attention to at the moment.

Do not lapse into a prayer life that is active only when great needs are present. Don't apply the "grease" of prayer only when something is squeaking loudly. Rather, be a man or woman of consistent prayer. James 5:16 tells us, "The effective, fervent prayer of a righteous man avails much." Romans 12:11, 12 admonishes us to be "fervent in spirit, serving the Lord; Rejoicing in hope, patient in tribulation, continuing steadfastly in prayer." Make a determination today to develop a steady prayer life and to become a person fervent in prayer.

.

NOTES:

PSALM 70
NEW KING JAMES VERSION

*¹ Make haste, O God, to deliver me!
Make haste to help me, O LORD!*

*² Let them be ashamed and confounded
Who seek my life;
Let them be turned back and confused
Who desire my hurt.
³ Let them be turned back because of their shame,
Who say, "Aha, aha!"*

*⁴ Let all those who seek You rejoice and be glad in You;
And let those who love Your salvation say continually,
"Let God be magnified!"*

*⁵ But I am poor and needy;
Make haste to me, O God!
You are my help and my deliverer;
O LORD, do not delay.*

56

CONFUSED
PSALM 70

I love Israel and the city of Jerusalem. Because of the particular ministry the Lord has assigned us to, Pam and I have been to Jerusalem many times. Being a traveler, I've driven in many cities in various countries, but no other city is as confusing to drive in as Jerusalem. Many cities are frustrating due to heavy traffic and overcrowding, but they are not necessarily confusing. If the streets of Jerusalem were completely empty, driving would still be confusing because the streets are laid out so strangely. Nothing, absolutely nothing, is square. I am usually pretty directional, but when I'm in Jerusalem, I am totally confused. Consequently, driving in Jerusalem is a very frustrating experience.

Frustration is a picture David painted in Psalm 70. While praying for relief from his adversaries, he prayed his enemies would be "turned back and confused." One translation uses the phrase "appalled and confused." David also prayed for confusion to come to his enemies in Psalm 35:4,26.

There are many examples in the Bible where God confused the enemies of His people. One example is recorded in Exodus 14. The Israelites had been in slavery for 430 years until Moses led them out of Egypt. On their voyage out of Egypt, they became trapped by the Red Sea on one side and Pharaoh's chariots on the other. God miraculously parted the Red Sea and the Israelites marched through on dry ground. The Egyptians were still in pursuit until God "troubled" (the word means confused) the army of Egyptians (Exodus 14:24). By taking away their clear thinking, He confused them, allowing them to mindlessly drive their chariots into a death trap. (See also devotion of Psalm 20.) Confusion prevented the Egyptians from reaching their goal of destroying Israel.

Perhaps you have a circumstance where it appears the enemy has the inside track. That is certainly how it looked to the Israelites in Exodus 14. But the Israelites' circumstance quickly turned once Pharaoh's army became confused. Just like driving in a city like Jerusalem, you can have an intended target, yet find it nearly impossible to get there. Your enemy may have targeted you, but confusion will prevent him from reaching his intended goal.

Pray, as did David, for God to confuse every plan that is laid against you. Pray that your enemy will never find an avenue by which to reach his intended goal. You enemy's confusion will be in favor of your victory.

PSALM 86
NEW KING JAMES VERSION

¹ *Bow down Your ear, O LORD, hear me;*
For I am poor and needy.
² *Preserve my life, for I am holy;*
You are my God;
Save Your servant who trusts in You!
³ *Be merciful to me, O Lord,*
For I cry to You all day long.
⁴ *Rejoice the soul of Your servant,*
For to You, O Lord, I lift up my soul.
⁵ *For You, Lord, are good, and ready to forgive,*
And abundant in mercy to all those who call upon You.

⁶ *Give ear, O LORD, to my prayer;*
And attend to the voice of my supplications.
⁷ *In the day of my trouble I will call upon You,*
For You will answer me.

⁸ *Among the gods there is none like You, O Lord;*
Nor are there any works like Your works.
⁹ *All nations whom You have made*
Shall come and worship before You, O Lord,
And shall glorify Your name.
¹⁰ *For You are great, and do wondrous things;*
You alone are God.

¹¹ *Teach me Your way, O LORD;*
I will walk in Your truth;
Unite my heart to fear Your name.
¹² *I will praise You, O Lord my God, with all my heart,*
And I will glorify Your name forevermore.
¹³ *For great is Your mercy toward me,*
And You have delivered my soul from the depths of Sheol.

¹⁴ *O God, the proud have risen against me,*
And a mob of violent men have sought my life,
And have not set You before them.

¹⁵ But You, O Lord, are a God full of compassion, and gracious,
Longsuffering and abundant in mercy and truth.

¹⁶ Oh, turn to me, and have mercy on me!
Give Your strength to Your servant,
And save the son of Your maidservant.
¹⁷ Show me a sign for good,
That those who hate me may see it and be ashamed,
Because You, LORD, have helped me and comforted me.

57

READY, SET, GO
PSALM 86

Psalm 86 is both a prayer for mercy and a meditation on the excellencies of the Lord. One of the wonderful truths contained in this psalm is the statement that God "is ready to forgive" (verse 5). I love that thought. God is ready to forgive! If you ask for God's forgiveness, He will set your name eternally in the Lamb's Book of Life (God's record book in Heaven, see Revelation 21:27). As a forgiven, blood-washed child of God, you will go to Heaven when you die. What a great and wonderful God He is!

"Getting ready" is something we do daily. We "get ready" to go to work, we "get ready" to go to school, we "get ready" to go to church, and so life goes. "Getting ready" involves planning. My wife knows how long it takes her to get ready to go out for dinner. She plans her time to get ready. Because God made His plans a long time ago to get ready, forgiveness is already provided when we ask for it. There are no delays with God's forgiveness. He stays ready! There is never an occasion when God is not ready to forgive.

When you get ready, everything is set to go. You cannot go until you are ready. Well, I guess you could, but my wife won't. She is not going anywhere with her hair and makeup in a mess. Everything falls in line when you are ready.

God got ready to forgive us even before Jesus went to the cross. He decided a long time ago to forgive us and had picked the perfect time to present redemption's fulfillment. The Bible says, "But when the fullness of the time had come (when the right time came), God sent forth His Son, born of a woman, born under the law, to redeem those who were under the law (that's us), that we might receive the adoption as sons. And because you are sons, God has sent forth the Spirit of His Son into your hearts, crying out, 'Abba, Father!' Therefore you are no longer a slave but a son, and if a son, then an heir of God through Christ" (Galatians 4:4-7). You are not a slave, but rather a son or daughter of God!

When my children come from out of town, they do not stay in a hotel. They stay in my house. That's what God plans for us to do. God put everything in place so we could be part of His kingdom. He got ready, so that when we ask forgiveness for us our sins, He would set our names in the Book of Life. With our name recorded there, it is certain we will go to the house He has prepared for us in Heaven (John 14:2,3).

PSALM 95
NEW KING JAMES VERSION

¹ Oh come, let us sing to the LORD!
Let us shout joyfully to the Rock of our salvation.
² Let us come before His presence with thanksgiving;
Let us shout joyfully to Him with psalms.
³ For the LORD is the great God,
And the great King above all gods.
⁴ In His hand are the deep places of the earth;
The heights of the hills are His also.
⁵ The sea is His, for He made it;
And His hands formed the dry land.

⁶ Oh come, let us worship and bow down;
Let us kneel before the LORD our Maker.
⁷ For He is our God,
And we are the people of His pasture,
And the sheep of His hand.

Today, if you will hear His voice:
⁸ "Do not harden your hearts, as in the rebellion,
As in the day of trial in the wilderness,
⁹ When your fathers tested Me;
They tried Me, though they saw My work.
¹⁰ For forty years I was grieved with that generation,
And said, 'It is a people who go astray in their hearts,
And they do not know My ways.'
¹¹ So I swore in My wrath,
'They shall not enter My rest.' "

58

THE KEY TO EVERYTHING
PSALM 95

Keys are things that control our lives in many ways. Try losing your car keys or your house keys and you will quickly see what I mean. One time I locked my keys in my car with the car running. Brilliant, huh? That definitely changed my itinerary for the afternoon.

I believe Psalm 95 contains a great key to the blessing of God upon our lives. It is the key to everything in God's kingdom. The key is named obedience.

There is an old song titled "Trust and Obey." The fact is you cannot obey someone you do not trust. If you do not trust them, you will not follow their command. The key to obeying God is trusting Him.

In Psalm 95:8-10, David focused on what happened to Israel when they refused to obey God. God miraculously led them from Egypt. After performing ten astonishing miracles before Pharaoh, He parted the Red Sea and drowned the Egyptian army in it. (See Exodus 14.) He made the bitter waters sweet in Exodus 15, sent them bread from heaven in Exodus 16, and provided water from a rock in Exodus 17. How could they not trust Him? Evidently they did not, even after observing miracle upon miracle in that first year after leaving Egypt. God finally led them to Canaan, the Land of Promise, but they refused to enter. There can only be one reason – they did not trust Him.

Trust is not the result of seeing a bunch of miracles. Trust is a decision. You must decide whether or not you believe God is a good God and true to his Word. Since I believe He is good and faithful, it is easy for me to trust Him. If He tells me to do something, it is not hard because I trust Him. He will not lead me on a path to destruction, and He will always lead me to safety.

The Israelites died in the wilderness because they hardened their hearts (Psalm 95:8) and went astray (Psalm 95:10). God had a completely different plan for them. Because God never forces His plan on us, we are free to choose obedience or disobedience. As the song goes, *I choose to trust and obey, for there's no other way, to be happy in Jesus, but to trust and obey*. That's the key to everything with God.

NOTES:

PSALM 101
NEW KING JAMES VERSION

[1] *I will sing of mercy and justice;*
To You, O LORD, I will sing praises.

[2] *I will behave wisely in a perfect way.*
Oh, when will You come to me?
I will walk within my house with a perfect heart.

[3] *I will set nothing wicked before my eyes;*
I hate the work of those who fall away;
It shall not cling to me.
[4] *A perverse heart shall depart from me;*
I will not know wickedness.

[5] *Whoever secretly slanders his neighbor,*
Him I will destroy;
The one who has a haughty look and a proud heart,
Him I will not endure.

[6] *My eyes shall be on the faithful of the land,*
That they may dwell with me;
He who walks in a perfect way,
He shall serve me.
[7] *He who works deceit shall not dwell within my house;*
He who tells lies shall not continue in my presence.
[8] *Early I will destroy all the wicked of the land,*
That I may cut off all the evildoers from the city of the LORD.

59

BE A GOOD BOY
PSALM 101

Before children leave the house, parents normally admonish them to "Be a good boy!" or "Be a good girl!" Most children benefit from these reminders. Of course, if kids misbehave in their parents' presence, discipline is normally administered. Similarly, God admonishes us to walk according to His statutes and corrects us when we miss it. Just like an earthly parent, God in His goodness corrects us because He loves us.

Our Heavenly Father expects us to mature in Him and make good decisions without Him constantly reminding us. Meditating Psalm 101 will help you with those choices. I encourage you to read and mediate this entire psalm. It is an important passage for successful Christian living. In most of our devotions, I have chosen just one Scripture or theme to focus on, primarily to keep them from being lengthy. This psalm, however, should be looked at verse by verse. Let's look at the commitment and choices King David made:

- David consciously praised God for His mercy and justice (verse 1). Where would we be without them? Lamentations 3:22,23 says, "Through the Lord's mercies we are not consumed, Because His compassions fail not. They are new every morning; great is Your faithfulness."
- David determined to "behave wisely in a blameless way" (verse 2). The Amplified Bible says, "I will walk within my house in my integrity and with a blameless heart." May that be our goal today and every day. It would certainly remove

a lot of heartache from the world and from many of our relationships.

- It has been said "the eyes are the window to the soul." The commitment to remove evil from our eyes will prevent many from committing a multitude of sins. We live in a world that will fill our eyes and minds with every form of lewdness. It is everywhere we turn. Things will come across our eyes in this world, but we can choose to immediately look away. We can't keep birds from flying over our head, but we can keep them from building a nest in our hair!

- We can also make the choice to not intentionally look at anything evil. In a world filled with pornography, this is a choice we must make for successful Christian living. All of us are human, including this author. We are capable of sinning. If you have a challenge in this area, I have good news today. There is help if you do two things: repent (turn away from) and make this commitment like David (verse 3). God will help you be strong in the areas you are weak. As stated earlier, God's compassion does not fail and is new every morning. Great is God's faithfulness, and He will help you be faithful.

- David committed in verse 4 to "not know wickedness." The Amplified Bible says, "I will know no evil person or thing."

- Choose friends who are not proud and do not even have a haughty look. Choose friends who do not slander. This means people who are not malicious, false, or defamatory (verse 5). In verse 6, David admonished choosing friends who are faithful and have a blameless heart. You will never find a perfect friend, but you can choose people with a good heart. They are the ones you want to speak into your life.

- I had a personal experience with verse 7. For many years my wife, Pam, and I have ministered in Eastern Europe and the Middle East. In one country where we maintain an office, we had an employee who concerned me. His actions said he was struggling in his walk with Christ. One day, I was riding with him and heard him lie to another man. Of course, I was troubled. I sincerely prayed, Lord, what should I do? He led me to this Scripture: "He who works deceit shall not dwell within my house; He who tells lies shall not continue in My presence." One of the most painful things I ever did was to release this man. Through the years, he had become almost like family to us. He is still my friend, and I love him today as much as ever. After the Lord showed me this, I felt I needed to quickly respond. In Psalm 101:8 David said, "Early...I will cut off evildoers." Perhaps the decision to release my employee helped that man examine himself.

David had to make decisions. He had a kingdom to rule. With all the business and life decisions we have to make, we need guidelines. If you are in a business position of leadership or own your own business, believe God to surround you with people who have a good heart. There are many people who do not profess Christ as Savior (yet), but they have a good heart. They do not lie or slander. I pray God will surround your life with friends and business associates who will encourage you and lend to your success.

Pray this prayer: *Lord, I praise You for Your mercy and justice. I confess Jesus Christ as my Savior and daily receive Your mercy and compassion. Thank You! As You help me, I commit to purity. I will set nothing wicked before my eyes. I will live a blameless life to the best of my ability. Help me choose my friends wisely. Fill my workplace with those who have a pure heart. Thank You for the strength You give me today to live according to Your Word. Amen.*

PSALM 103
NEW KING JAMES VERSION

¹ *Bless the LORD, O my soul;*
And all that is within me, bless His holy name!
² *Bless the LORD, O my soul,*
And forget not all His benefits:
³ *Who forgives all your iniquities,*
Who heals all your diseases,
⁴ *Who redeems your life from destruction,*
Who crowns you with lovingkindness and tender mercies,
⁵ *Who satisfies your mouth with good things,*
So that your youth is renewed like the eagle's.

⁶ *The LORD executes righteousness*
And justice for all who are oppressed.
⁷ *He made known His ways to Moses,*
His acts to the children of Israel.
⁸ *The LORD is merciful and gracious,*
Slow to anger, and abounding in mercy.
⁹ *He will not always strive with us,*
Nor will He keep His anger forever.
¹⁰ *He has not dealt with us according to our sins,*
Nor punished us according to our iniquities.

¹¹ *For as the heavens are high above the earth,*
So great is His mercy toward those who fear Him;
¹² *As far as the east is from the west,*
So far has He removed our transgressions from us.
¹³ *As a father pities his children,*
So the LORD pities those who fear Him.
¹⁴ *For He knows our frame;*
He remembers that we are dust.

¹⁵ *As for man, his days are like grass;*
As a flower of the field, so he flourishes.
¹⁶ *For the wind passes over it, and it is gone,*
And its place remembers it no more.
¹⁷ *But the mercy of the LORD is from everlasting to everlasting*
On those who fear Him,

And His righteousness to children's children,
¹⁸ To such as keep His covenant,
And to those who remember His commandments to do them.

¹⁹ The LORD has established His throne in heaven,
And His kingdom rules over all.

²⁰ Bless the LORD, you His angels,
Who excel in strength, who do His word,
Heeding the voice of His word.
²¹ Bless the LORD, all you His hosts,
You ministers of His, who do His pleasure.
²² Bless the LORD, all His works,
In all places of His dominion.

Bless the LORD, O my soul!

60

TIE A STRING AROUND
YOUR FINGER
PSALM 103

The human brain possesses amazing capacity. Scientists say that we can store as many as 600 memories per second without strain for a lifetime of seventy-five years. That would be almost 142 billion memories stored in the average life. You may be thinking, "If that is true, why is it easy to forget important things?" How many men have forgotten one of the most important days in their life, their wedding anniversary? I hope that never happens to you. Tie a string around your finger!

Some things are easier to remember than others. I had a friend tell me one time that she had the hardest time memorizing Scripture while other things were not as difficult. The reason is pretty obvious. Jesus taught in His parables that Satan will come quickly to steal the Word from us. (See Matthew 13:19.)

In Psalm 103:2 David said, "Bless the Lord, O my soul, And forget not all His benefits." This psalm focuses on many of the benefits God extends to His people. Before I discuss the benefits listed in this psalm, I want you to determine a way to help you remember them.

This is a Biblical principle. I have dear Jewish friends who explained to me why God told the Israelites to make tassels on the corners of their garments. (See Numbers 15:37-41.) God wants His people to have a constant reminder of His commandments and to obey them. If we have reminders throughout the day, we are much more prone to obey the commandments than if we ignore them. Obviously, I don't wear tassels on my garments, but I do carry small Scripture cards in my wallet. Sometimes in the middle of the day, I pull them out and read them. What an uplift that brings to my spirit! Now, let's take a look at some of those benefits listed in Psalm 103:

- He forgives all your iniquities
- He heals all your diseases
- He redeems your life from destruction
- He crowns you with loving kindness and tender mercies
- He satisfies you with good things
- He renews your youth
- He executes righteousness and justice on your behalf
- He is gracious, slow to anger, and abounds in mercy
- He doesn't punish you according to your sins
- He removes your transgressions as far as the east is from the west.

Psalm 103:1 says, "Bless the Lord, O my soul, And all that is within me, bless His holy name!" Take a moment right now and thank Him that your sins are gone forever. Throughout your day, remember His amazing benefits!

Psalm 108
New King James Version

¹ O God, my heart is steadfast;
I will sing and give praise, even with my glory.
² Awake, lute and harp!
I will awaken the dawn.
³ I will praise You, O LORD, among the peoples,
And I will sing praises to You among the nations.
⁴ For Your mercy is great above the heavens,
And Your truth reaches to the clouds.

⁵ Be exalted, O God, above the heavens,
And Your glory above all the earth;
⁶ That Your beloved may be delivered,
Save with Your right hand, and hear me.

⁷ God has spoken in His holiness:
"I will rejoice;
I will divide Shechem
And measure out the Valley of Succoth.
⁸ Gilead is Mine; Manasseh is Mine;
Ephraim also is the helmet for My head;
Judah is My lawgiver.
⁹ Moab is My washpot;
Over Edom I will cast My shoe;
Over Philistia I will triumph."

¹⁰ Who will bring me into the strong city?
Who will lead me to Edom?
¹¹ Is it not You, O God, who cast us off?
And You, O God, who did not go out with our armies?
¹² Give us help from trouble,
For the help of man is useless.
¹³ Through God we will do valiantly,
For it is He who shall tread down our enemies.

61

IN THE ZONE
PSALM 108

David said in Psalm 108:1, "O God, my heart is steadfast (zoned in); I will sing and give praise, even with my glory." So many things throughout the day compel us to forget God. We have to work at being God-conscious. David made a determination to live in the zone, the zone of constant awareness of God. In this place of steadfast focus, circumstances are not allowed to deter people from praising God. In another psalm David said, "Seven times a day I will praise the Lord." Now that is being zoned in, or locked in to God. In the face of intense challenges, David determined to live in that zone. He knew that God alone was his source of help.

My wife, Pam, and I faced a major challenge many years ago. She had been ill for four years. Doctors could not find the problem. (See Psalm 22 devotion.) One day, a doctor walked into her hospital room and said, "I have good news and bad news. The good news is that we have found what is wrong with you. It is a very rare blood disorder called Familiar Mediterranean Fever. (Pam is Italian.) The bad news is that there is no cure." Since this doctor was a Christian, he went on to say, "Of course we know there is an answer, it is just not found in medical science. We will pray and believe God to heal you."

This story might explain David's prayer in verse 12: "Give us help from trouble, for the help of man is useless." The doctor's help was not useless, and he answered a lot of questions. For four years Pam had been to various doctors and hospitals. They could see the symptoms in her blood but could not understand where it was coming from. Her blood count would be radically off. Because our blood cycles, she would be extremely ill for about one week and then get better for about three or four weeks until the blood completed its cycle. While everyone was frustrated, Pam's health continued to deteriorate.

I am obviously not a doctor, evidenced by my feeble explanation, but you get the point. Man's help was useless in solving the problem. The doctor could diagnose the disease, but he could not fix it. We were grateful for the diagnosis, because it provided a specific name we could take to God in prayer. We are grateful to the Lord that He did heal her soon after, and she has been well for twenty-five years.

Friends and family were a great help during this four-year ordeal. We never would have made it without them. In this psalm, David was not saying man is of no help at all. He was saying man cannot deal the fatal blow to the enemy, only God can. God will use people in all of our lives. Thankfully, we are not on this planet alone. If you have a major problem to deal with, do what you can and let God do what you cannot. I think that is the message of the psalmist. Stay in the zone today of praising God, and know He is the problem solver.

NOTES:

PSALM 109
NEW KING JAMES VERSION

¹ Do not keep silent,
O God of my praise!
² For the mouth of the wicked and the mouth of the deceitful
Have opened against me;
They have spoken against me with a lying tongue.
³ They have also surrounded me with words of hatred,
And fought against me without a cause.
⁴ In return for my love they are my accusers,
But I give myself to prayer.
⁵ Thus they have rewarded me evil for good,
And hatred for my love.

⁶ Set a wicked man over him,
And let an accuser stand at his right hand.
⁷ When he is judged, let him be found guilty,
And let his prayer become sin.
⁸ Let his days be few,
And let another take his office.
⁹ Let his children be fatherless,
And his wife a widow.
¹⁰ Let his children continually be vagabonds, and beg;
Let them seek their bread also from their desolate places.
¹¹ Let the creditor seize all that he has,
And let strangers plunder his labor.
¹² Let there be none to extend mercy to him,
Nor let there be any to favor his fatherless children.
¹³ Let his posterity be cut off,
And in the generation following let their name be blotted out.

¹⁴ Let the iniquity of his fathers be remembered before the LORD,
And let not the sin of his mother be blotted out.
¹⁵ Let them be continually before the LORD,
That He may cut off the memory of them from the earth;
¹⁶ Because he did not remember to show mercy,
But persecuted the poor and needy man,
That he might even slay the broken in heart.

¹⁷ As he loved cursing, so let it come to him;
As he did not delight in blessing, so let it be far from him.
¹⁸ As he clothed himself with cursing as with his garment,
So let it enter his body like water,
And like oil into his bones.
¹⁹ Let it be to him like the garment which covers him,
And for a belt with which he girds himself continually.
²⁰ Let this be the LORD's reward to my accusers,
And to those who speak evil against my person.

²¹ But You, O GOD the Lord,
Deal with me for Your name's sake;
Because Your mercy is good, deliver me.
²² For I am poor and needy,
And my heart is wounded within me.
²³ I am gone like a shadow when it lengthens;
I am shaken off like a locust.
²⁴ My knees are weak through fasting,
And my flesh is feeble from lack of fatness.
²⁵ I also have become a reproach to them;
When they look at me, they shake their heads.

²⁶ Help me, O LORD my God!
Oh, save me according to Your mercy,
²⁷ That they may know that this is Your hand—
That You, LORD, have done it!
²⁸ Let them curse, but You bless;
When they arise, let them be ashamed,
But let Your servant rejoice.
²⁹ Let my accusers be clothed with shame,
And let them cover themselves
with their own disgrace as with a mantle.

³⁰ I will greatly praise the LORD with my mouth;
Yes, I will praise Him among the multitude.
³¹ For He shall stand at the right hand of the poor,
To save him from those who condemn him.

62

SKIN AND BONES
PSALM 109

Have you ever fasted? I venture to guess that some who read this have not. That does not mean you are unspiritual. It may mean you have missed a great opportunity to draw closer to God. Fasting does not change God, but it does place you in a position to hear more easily from Him.

Man is a three-part being: spirit, soul, and body. (See 1 Thessalonians 5:23.) We are spirit beings who possess a soul and live in a body. Our spirit is the eternal part of us, while the soul is the mind, will, and emotions. The body…well, it is something I have trouble with from time to time. The aging process causes it to function less and less as it once did. (Don't laugh – you are no different!)

We tend to spend way more time on our body than we do our soul and spirit, and yet, the body still betrays us. The body is dying from the moment we are born. The spirit is just the opposite. The spirit man is not perishing, but rather getting started! We are going to live forever. Scripture teaches that in the resurrection we will have a new body. So why do we spend exhaustive amounts of time on the body and not the spirit? It is probably because human nature is to think of now.

Now is the time to think about the spirit. We should take care of our bodies, because they are the temple of the Holy Spirit (1 Corinthians 6:19). However, the greatest emphasis needs to be placed on our spirit man. Fasting and prayer allow us to discipline our flesh in order to focus on our spirit.

As you read Psalm 109, don't focus on David's lengthy prayer about his enemies. His prayer might seem cruel, but it wasn't. To understand David's perspective, you need to look back on his experiences and find out where he was coming from. Here, David had been falsely accused by people he had treated well. While reading this psalm, focus instead on David's decision. He was facing a very difficult circumstance, but he knew God was the only answer.

Through this psalm, we can see David's response to his situation was to fast and pray. As he drew close to God, he said, "In return for my love they are my accusers, but I give myself to prayer" (verse 4). In verse 24 he said, "My knees are weak through fasting, and my flesh is feeble from lack of fatness." From that verse, it seems David's body fat had decreased from going on a long fast. As a result of fasting, his appearance could have been skin and bones.

If the thought of fasting intimidates you, it may be because you've heard of someone going on a forty-day fast. My personal opinion is that such a fast should be directed by the Lord, especially if done totally without food. In fact, the New Testament does not record any forty-day fast, except for the fast Jesus experienced in the wilderness. For further study on fasting, there are many great books available on this topic. If you've never fasted, allow me to suggest that sometime you give up one meal and use the twenty minutes you would spend eating for prayer. You may find spiritual food better than natural food.

PSALM 110
NEW KING JAMES VERSION

¹ The LORD said to my Lord,
"Sit at My right hand,
Till I make Your enemies Your footstool."
² The LORD shall send the rod of Your strength out of Zion.
Rule in the midst of Your enemies!

³ Your people shall be volunteers
In the day of Your power;
In the beauties of holiness, from the womb of the morning,
You have the dew of Your youth.
⁴ The LORD has sworn
And will not relent,
"You are a priest forever
According to the order of Melchizedek."

⁵ The Lord is at Your right hand;
He shall execute kings in the day of His wrath.
⁶ He shall judge among the nations,
He shall fill the places with dead bodies,
He shall execute the heads of many countries.
⁷ He shall drink of the brook by the wayside;
Therefore He shall lift up the head.

63

I'M NOT KENNY G
PSALM 110

The first verse of Psalm 110 intrigues me: "The Lord said to my Lord, (this would be God talking to Jesus) 'Sit at My right hand, Till I make Your enemies Your footstool.'" That is sort of like saying, "Sit down and relax, don't worry about your enemies. While you are sitting down and not worrying about them, I'll be making them into a footstool for you." Yes, I have enjoyed a little word play here, but I am not far from the truth. It would be great if we could learn to live that way, simply turning everything over to God and not worrying about anything. I encourage you to try it today.

There are many organizations that are successful largely due to the benefit of volunteers. Our churches would possibly be at the top of the list. The church we attend has hundreds of people that volunteer their time, talent, and treasure. Without volunteers, there would be no church as we know it today. Churches are just one of many organizations that thrive because people believe in them and want to be a part.

To "volunteer" something, you have to possess it first. You cannot give time you do not have. However, all of us have twenty-four hours every day. There is no exception. You cannot use a talent you do not possess. All of us have talent. God placed gifts and callings within all of us. According to Romans 11:29, "The gifts and the calling of God are irrevocable." The Bible even tells us to "stir up the gift which is within you" (2 Timothy 1:6). If we get lax in our commitment, we are to "stir" ourselves, or get out and do something. Sometimes we do not even know we can do something until we try.

I have always wanted to play the saxophone. A few years ago, I was ministering in a church pastored by a close friend who is a tremendous saxophonist. I told him the saxophone was my favorite instrument and had always wished I had learned to play. He told me to meet him the next morning at the church. When I arrived, he had two saxophones. Within an hour he taught me to play a song. Now, don't get the wrong impression – I'm not Kenny G. (For those of you unaware, Kenny G is a very famous saxophonist.) My point is I could do something I didn't know I could do. Without putting forth the effort, I never would have known I could learn how to play.

Volunteering requires putting forth effort. I challenge you to look for a place to volunteer – there is great reward in giving of yourself or something you have. If you're not already a volunteer at your church, find a place and plug in. You can serve as an usher, greeter, or in lawn care. There are a host of places in which you can be a blessing.

When you volunteer, you may discover a talent you did not know you had. You will find joy because there is great joy in serving others. All of us have twenty-four hours in a day. Although most of us live busy lives, I trust you will never get too be busy to find a few moments to make a difference in someone else's life. Become a volunteer and make a difference for someone else today.

NOTES:

PSALM 122
NEW KING JAMES VERSION

¹ I was glad when they said to me,
"Let us go into the house of the LORD."
² Our feet have been standing
Within your gates, O Jerusalem!

³ Jerusalem is built
As a city that is compact together,
⁴ Where the tribes go up,
The tribes of the LORD,
To the Testimony of Israel,
To give thanks to the name of the LORD.
⁵ For thrones are set there for judgment,
The thrones of the house of David.

⁶ Pray for the peace of Jerusalem:
"May they prosper who love you.
⁷ Peace be within your walls,
Prosperity within your palaces."
⁸ For the sake of my brethren and companions,
I will now say, "Peace be within you."
⁹ Because of the house of the LORD our God
I will seek your good.

64

"P"
PSALM 122

Psalm 122 contains three significant words on which I would like to focus. Found in verses 7 and 8, these words all start with the letter "P" – prayer, peace, and prosperity. Before looking at them, there is a great verse to read. Psalm 122:1 says, "I was glad when they said unto me, 'Let us go into the house of the Lord.'" David looked forward to going to the temple to worship God. In the Old Testament, the temple represented the place of the presence of God. Today, God's presence is always with us through faith in Jesus Christ as our Savior (See Ephesians 2:22.) We should be "glad" about that.

The statement in verse 1 also implies going to worship with other worshippers. I hope you are able to regularly worship with a good church family. It is very important for spiritual growth and maturity. If you do not have a church family, I encourage you to make it a serious consideration and pray for God to lead you to a good church home. Now, let's return to the letter "P."

Prayer is talked about a lot in this devotional because David was a man of prayer. This was a key element in him becoming "a man after God's own heart" (Acts 13:22). Becoming a person who regularly communes with God takes discipline and is another key to spiritual growth. Many things seem to fight us when we try to pray. For example, have you ever fallen asleep while praying? If you have, do not be condemned – most of us have drifted off during prayer at one time or another. When you wake up, simply pray some more. I would rather fall asleep while praying than worrying anyway. I once heard it said that some of the sweetest naps have been taken at an altar. We are also commanded to "pray for the peace of Jerusalem." Please take a moment and do so today.

Peace. Notice that David said "peace be within your walls." He was talking about Jerusalem here. Through the ages, this beautiful city – chosen by God – has been surrounded with turmoil, suffering a multitude of attacks. Yet, it remains stronger than ever today.

As I read this psalm today, I wondered if it could be symbolic of us. Do we not live in a world filled with unrest? The world is without peace and will be so until the Prince of Peace, Jesus, returns one day. But does that mean we have to live without peace in this world? No, emphatically no! You can have God's peace "within your walls." Your household and family can live in peace. That is God's desire for you. Your peace of mind and heart do not have to be decided by external factors, but by the inward, abiding peace of God. Regardless of the external factors, allow His peace to dwell within "the walls" of your heart and home today.

Prosperity. God wants us to be whole in every area and relation. God does not want His people to lack, but He does not want us to be self-consuming either. He wants us to be blessed (prosperous) so we can be a blessing to (prosper) others. (See Genesis 12:2.) When you read these final words for today, take a moment and ask God for His wisdom, guidance, counsel, and protection. He is the only One who can cause you to prosper.

NOTES:

PSALM 124
NEW KING JAMES VERSION

---

[1] *"If it had not been the LORD who was on our side,"*
Let Israel now say—
[2] *"If it had not been the LORD who was on our side,*
When men rose up against us,
[3] *Then they would have swallowed us alive,*
When their wrath was kindled against us;
[4] *Then the waters would have overwhelmed us,*
The stream would have gone over our soul;
[5] *Then the swollen waters*
Would have gone over our soul."

[6] *Blessed be the LORD,*
Who has not given us as prey to their teeth.
[7] *Our soul has escaped as a bird from the snare of the fowlers;*
The snare is broken, and we have escaped.
[8] *Our help is in the name of the LORD,*
Who made heaven and earth.

65

YOUR SIDE OF THE BALL
PSALM 124

In most sporting events there is an offense and a defense for each team. One team does its best to score while the other tries to stop them. In football, players generally specialize in either offense or defense. If you play football, you are probably familiar with the phrase "Which side of the ball do you play on?" This term simply means "Do you play offense or defense?" Many teams have an exceptional player who largely contributes to their success. In those cases, teams are glad to have this star player on their side of the ball. That is similar to what David was saying in Psalm 124:1: "If it had not been the Lord who was on our side…"

A team does not need a defense unless their opponent has an offense. David was describing his enemy as being very aggressive in his offense. In verse 3, he stated that without the Lord on our side we would be swallowed alive! That is a bit like a football game with the score 77-0. The great news is the Lord was on David's side, and He is on your side of the ball too.

Satan does have an offense and he wants to win. Great football teams scout their opponents and mark their strengths and weaknesses, after which they formulate a game plan. The Bible tells us that when the final score is tallied, Satan loses in a rout! Yet, we still have to play the game. While the game is going on, remember the Lord is on your side of the ball.

Jesus said in Matthew 16:18: "I will build My church, and the gates of Hades shall not prevail against it." Did you notice two things in that verse? First, Satan "shall not" win. Did you also notice Jesus said that Hell has gates? I find that interesting. In Bible times, cities were built inside walls for protection against invading armies. The walls had gates for entry and exit, which could be locked in times of warfare to complete the circle of defense. Gates were part of the defense.

In time of warfare, the city leaders would customarily meet at the city gates to form their battle strategy. Satan does that, but all his defensive scheming will not succeed against us. Ephesians 6:11 says, "Put on the whole armor of God, that you may be able to stand against the wiles of the devil. "Wiles" literally means "scheming." The devil schemes against you, but his schemes will not work in the end because – and I think you have this already – the Lord is on your side of the ball.

NOTES:

Psalm 131
New King James Version

[1] LORD, my heart is not haughty,
Nor my eyes lofty.
Neither do I concern myself with great matters,
Nor with things too profound for me.

[2] Surely I have calmed and quieted my soul,
Like a weaned child with his mother;
Like a weaned child is my soul within me.

[3] O Israel, hope in the LORD
From this time forth and forever.

66

OUT OF MY LEAGUE
PSALM 131

The first verse of Psalm 131 contains a very interesting thought. I am convinced David's experiences were much like our own. Occasionally, David had questions in life for which he couldn't find answers. Everyone faces times when answers to life's questions seem just out of reach.

I was blessed with a father-in-law who was one of the finest men to ever walk the earth. His name was Joe Calabrese. He was also my pastor from age twelve until five years after I married Pam. He was my mentor in ministry. Next to my own father, he was the most important man in the world to me.

On a Sunday morning, he was suddenly taken from this life at the young age of fifty-five. Of course, he went to a better place, but he left a large void. Now almost thirty years later, I still think of him often and miss him. Pam and I, along with many others, questioned "Why?" I am not sure anyone knows the answer.

Answers are something we like to get when we have disturbing, probing questions. I've had many questions God has answered. However, I still haven't found a satisfactory answer to the question regarding my father-in-law's death. I am certain that God answers our questions when He knows it is best to provide an answer. I am left to think He sometimes knows it is best to leave questions alone.

When God doesn't seem to be answering a question, His silence is probably suggesting we leave the question alone. Sometimes the answer may be beyond our ability to comprehend. Maybe we could not handle the answer in the way God would expect. It is information that is best for us to not have.

I am certain my comments are raising some questions. In no way am I implying I have the answer. I am saying God has the answer to all things, and it is up to His discretion as to whether or not it is best for us for Him to share it with us. It is His prerogative since He is the Source of all things.

In all His encompassing knowledge and wisdom, God is privy to every detail. That would include the secrets in the heart of another that is reserved for God and that person. I liken it to baseball. As a boy I loved to play. I could hit a fastball – but only in my league. No way could I hit a Major League fastball. The guys that play on television pitch it almost 100 miles per hour. Some people say that the most difficult thing in sports is to hit a 100 mph fastball. They are out of my league and in a league of their own.

I have come to the conclusion there are some things with God that are out of my league. Like David, I must not "concern...myself with matters too great for me" (verse 1). It is best to leave all things in the hands of God and say to Him, "I may not understand it, but I trust You."

NOTES:

PSALM 133
NEW KING JAMES VERSION

¹ Behold, how good and how pleasant it is
For brethren to dwell together in unity!

² It is like the precious oil upon the head,
Running down on the beard,
The beard of Aaron,
Running down on the edge of his garments.
³ It is like the dew of Hermon,
Descending upon the mountains of Zion;
For there the LORD commanded the blessing—
Life forevermore.

67

GOD SAYS, "WOW!"
PSALM 133

Psalm 133 has only three verses, yet it contains one of the most important messages in the Bible – the unity among believers. In this chapter, David used word pictures to describe the power and fruit of the unity of God's people. Unity is imperative to walking in the blessings of God.

While Satan divides and subtracts, God adds and multiplies. If we desire the benefit of God's added blessings and the multiplication of His favor in our lives, we must fight to walk in unity. Romans 12:18 says, "If it is possible, as much as depends on you, live peaceably with all men." Jesus prayed for this in Gethsemane, even as He prepared to go to the cross (John 17:21). Unity is that important.

When a group of people lay aside their differences and come together, focusing on the task at hand and understanding the assignment God has given them to accomplish His purpose, God says it is "good and pleasant" (verse 1). Our assignment is to make every effort to live in unity. According to verse 3, unity commands God's blessing. Psalm 133:2 says this unity "is like the precious oil upon the head, running down on the beard of Aaron." Oil symbolizes God's anointing, or His empowerment. Each of us should desire that in our lives. Anointing also refers to a spiritual process in which the Holy Spirit empowers a person's heart and mind with God's truth and love (1 John 2:20, 27).

Jesus stated in the Sermon on the Mount in Matthew 5:9, "Blessed are the peacemakers, For they shall be called the Sons of God." He did not say blessed are the peacekeepers. He said peacemakers. Those who make or create peace are blessed. Sometimes you have to fight to make or establish peace. That is what soldiers do. In many places of the world today, our soldiers are fighting to establish peace. Where no peace exists, they fight for its existence.

Sometimes, to have peace in our lives, we have to fight through feelings of injustice, unforgiveness, and rejection. In matters involving others, we must at times fight past the feeling of "I am right." In most cases of strife, before restitution can come, one person usually chooses to take the high road and initiate bringing the strife to an end. Often, the issue over which the fight exists is not that important anyway. Families have needlessly been shattered over fighting about inheriting Grandma's glass dish. Who cares? Grandma doesn't care because she is in Heaven. If she could talk back to you, she would say, "It's just a dish!"

The first word of this psalm in English is "Behold." The word carries a sense of amazement. Rick Renner once said that "behold" is not the most perfect translation of the Hebrew word used in original manuscripts. He stated that a closer word would be "Wow." It brings the Lord great happiness and satisfaction when He sees His people standing in complete agreement. When God's people choose to live in unity and walk in love, God says, "Wow!" Could that be because it does not happen as often as it should?

As you meditate on this psalm today, may I encourage you to search your heart and ask God if there is some place you need to be a peacemaker. When you bring peace and enable others to come together in unity, God will look down and say, "Wow!"

NOTES:

PSALM 138
NEW KING JAMES VERSION

[1] I will praise You with my whole heart;
Before the gods I will sing praises to You.
[2] I will worship toward Your holy temple,
And praise Your name
For Your lovingkindness and Your truth;
For You have magnified Your word above all Your name.
[3] In the day when I cried out, You answered me,
And made me bold with strength in my soul.

[4] All the kings of the earth shall praise You, O LORD,
When they hear the words of Your mouth.
[5] Yes, they shall sing of the ways of the LORD,
For great is the glory of the LORD.
[6] Though the LORD is on high,
Yet He regards the lowly;
But the proud He knows from afar.

[7] Though I walk in the midst of trouble, You will revive me;
You will stretch out Your hand
Against the wrath of my enemies,
And Your right hand will save me.
[8] The LORD will perfect that which concerns me;
Your mercy, O LORD, endures forever;
Do not forsake the works of Your hands..

68

BOATS AND GODS
PSALM 138

This psalm begins with "I will praise You with my whole heart; Before the gods I will sing praises to You." David was saying he would worship the one True God, in the face of all other gods. The wording strongly suggests that the psalmist is in a foreign, idolatrous land. This reminds me of the story told in Daniel 6. Daniel was thrown into a lion's den because he worshipped God in the face of the gods.

One must understand the tactic of Satan. He will do anything in his power to get us to worship anything except God. Putting anything ahead of God is idolatry. We live in a world filled with gods. In America the gods are not idols and statues, but rather people, material possessions, and various forms of entertainment. It's easy to place more importance on a person or object than on God.

My family loves to go to the lake. I have been water skiing since the age five. We had a nice ski boat a few years ago. One day, God distinctly spoke to me to sell the boat and give the money to a specific ministry. So, I sold the boat and gave the money as He directed. Later, I realized the whole process was about more than just giving the boat away. I was being tested. (See devotion on Psalm 11.) This was my opportunity to keep an "idol" from being erected in my life. Again, idolatry is anything more important to you than God and His plan for your life. God was not against our family having a boat. In fact, in the end we got a little bit better one. What He wanted was for us to have a boat but the boat not to have us. You see, if I had allowed it, boats and gods could have become the same thing.

The world we live in is not a lot different than the world of David's day. There are idols everywhere we turn. People worship sports, jobs, careers, cars, boats, motorcycles, homes, boyfriends, spouses, musicians... Anything that gets in front of our worship of the True God becomes idolatry. So, don't allow "gods" to be a part of your life!

Now, I do not believe God is against your having a nice car or home or boat. Just make sure the ownership of them does not have more importance than your relationship with God. Most people would have a closer relationship with God if they spent as much time with Him as they did washing their car and boat. Ouch! As I write, I am talking to myself as well.

For today's devotion, let's start with examining ourselves to see if we find any idols that need to be brought down (1 Corinthians 11:28). If any idols are present in your life, deal with them the way God shows you. Then, do as did David. He worshipped his God in the face of the gods. Worship is an action. Your worship will tell God that He, and He alone, is first place in your life.

NOTES:

PSALM 139
NEW KING JAMES VERSION

¹ O LORD, You have searched me and known me.
² You know my sitting down and my rising up;
You understand my thought afar off.
³ You comprehend my path and my lying down,
And are acquainted with all my ways.
⁴ For there is not a word on my tongue,
But behold, O LORD, You know it altogether.
⁵ You have hedged me behind and before,
And laid Your hand upon me.
⁶ Such knowledge is too wonderful for me;
It is high, I cannot attain it.

⁷ Where can I go from Your Spirit?
Or where can I flee from Your presence?
⁸ If I ascend into heaven, You are there;
If I make my bed in hell, behold, You are there.
⁹ If I take the wings of the morning,
And dwell in the uttermost parts of the sea,
¹⁰ Even there Your hand shall lead me,
And Your right hand shall hold me.
¹¹ If I say, "Surely the darkness shall fall on me,"
Even the night shall be light about me;
¹² Indeed, the darkness shall not hide from You,
But the night shines as the day;
The darkness and the light are both alike to You.

¹³ For You formed my inward parts;
You covered me in my mother's womb.
¹⁴ I will praise You, for I am fearfully and wonderfully made;
Marvelous are Your works,
And that my soul knows very well.
¹⁵ My frame was not hidden from You,
When I was made in secret,
And skillfully wrought in the lowest parts of the earth.
¹⁶ Your eyes saw my substance, being yet unformed.
And in Your book they all were written,

The days fashioned for me,
When as yet there were none of them.

[17] How precious also are Your thoughts to me, O God!
How great is the sum of them!
[18] If I should count them, they would be more in number than the sand;
When I awake, I am still with You.

[19] Oh, that You would slay the wicked, O God!
Depart from me, therefore, you bloodthirsty men.
[20] For they speak against You wickedly;
Your enemies take Your name in vain.
[21] Do I not hate them, O LORD, who hate You?
And do I not loathe those who rise up against You?
22 I hate them with perfect hatred;
I count them my enemies.

[23] Search me, O God, and know my heart;
Try me, and know my anxieties;
[24] And see if there is any wicked way in me,
And lead me in the way everlasting.

69

HE DOES NOT THINK LIKE ME
PSALM 139

Sometimes when I am in deep thought or daydreaming, I get a faraway look in my eyes. When I'm like this, my wife will ask, "What are you thinking about?" Her question normally jolts me out of my reverie and brings me back to the present moment.

Although God is very near us, sometimes we feel He is far away. Usually those feelings pop up when we are experiencing something in our lives we do not understand. During those moments, we would like to ask God, "What are You thinking about? Do You know what is going on in my life?" His answer to that is partly found in Isaiah 55:8, 9: "'For My thoughts are not your thoughts, Nor are your ways My ways,' says the Lord. 'For as the heavens are higher than the earth, So are My ways higher than your ways, And My thoughts than your thoughts.'" In other words, God doesn't think like me.

Our two children were married six weeks apart. A few months after their weddings, their mother asked them what had been their biggest surprise or adjustment. Natalie's answer was, "Learning that he does not think like me." Welcome to the world of the union of man and woman! That may be one reason God made Eve. He may have thought, "I need this man to think a little differently." Many times, my wife helps me see things I usually miss from a man's perspective.

Since we cannot humanly understand how God thinks, we must go to His Word to gain perspective on what He is thinking. Take a look at

Psalm 139:17, 18: "How precious are Your thoughts to me, O God! How great is the sum of them! If I should count them, they would be more in number than the sand; When I awake, I am still with You."

Let's go back to the husband and wife analogy. Men and women were not created to think alike. We are to complement each other. Although I do not understand how my wife thinks, I am convinced she loves me unconditionally and thinks good thoughts toward me. Sometimes when I travel, she puts a note in my suitcase. When I arrive at my destination and find her note as I unpack, I know I'm in her thoughts. I don't need my wife to think like me, but I do need her to think about me. Because Pam loves me, I know her thoughts are good.

Obviously, you do not want God to think like you. If He did, we would all be in big trouble! He knows every detail and circumstance surrounding you – especially, the things you cannot see. All you need is for God to think about you. Because He loves you unconditionally, His thoughts about you are always good thoughts. If He is thinking about you, everything is going to be all right, even the things you do not understand. He knows all the details. Since He is thinking about you, why not let Him handle your life? According to Psalm 139:17, 18, we know we are always on His mind. Verse 18 says, "When I awake, I am still with You." So, cast your cares on Him and sleep well!

PSALM 140
NEW KING JAMES VERSION

¹ *Deliver me, O LORD, from evil men;*
Preserve me from violent men,
² *Who plan evil things in their hearts;*
They continually gather together for war.
³ *They sharpen their tongues like a serpent;*
The poison of asps is under their lips. Selah

⁴ *Keep me, O LORD, from the hands of the wicked;*
Preserve me from violent men,
Who have purposed to make my steps stumble.
⁵ *The proud have hidden a snare for me, and cords;*
They have spread a net by the wayside;
They have set traps for me. Selah

⁶ *I said to the LORD: "You are my God;*
Hear the voice of my supplications, O LORD.
⁷ *O GOD the Lord, the strength of my salvation,*
You have covered my head in the day of battle.
⁸ *Do not grant, O LORD, the desires of the wicked;*
Do not further his wicked scheme,
Lest they be exalted. Selah

⁹ *"As for the head of those who surround me,*
Let the evil of their lips cover them;
¹⁰ *Let burning coals fall upon them;*
Let them be cast into the fire,
Into deep pits, that they rise not up again.
¹¹ *Let not a slanderer be established in the earth;*
Let evil hunt the violent man to overthrow him."

¹² *I know that the LORD will maintain*
The cause of the afflicted, and justice for the poor.
¹³ *Surely the righteous shall give thanks to Your name;*
The upright shall dwell in Your presence.

70

SNAKE POISON
PSALM 140

In Psalm 140:3 David says of evil and violent people, "They sharpen their tongues like a serpent; The poison of asps is under their lips." In other words, these people are like snake poison. Personally, I don't like snakes. I have a brother who had a "pet" rattlesnake for several years. He lives in south Texas where rattlesnakes are abundant. One day, he caught one and decided to keep it, feed it, and watch it grow. Grow it did – into one of the ugliest things I have ever seen.

Without immediate treatment, a rattlesnake bite can kill a person very easily. Although my brother's "pet" was large, a small rattlesnake can do just as much damage. That is kind of like people – they don't have to be very large to do a lot of damage. In fact, the Epistle of James tells us one of the smallest members of the body, the tongue, can do the most damage (James 3:3-12).

For contemplation in devotions today, let's consider three things. First, ask yourself, "Am I allowing my tongue to be the poison of a serpent?" A little self-examination never hurts. Ask God to help you control your tongue. Control it at work when you want to reply to a sharp word with a sharp word. Control it at home when you are tempted to pour out complaints on end. I have even had to bite my tongue a time or two, and later was glad I did. The physical pain of biting my tongue was much less than the emotional pain that would have been caused by spiteful words.

Secondly, please consider the question, "Am I hanging out with snakes?" We become like the people with whom we associate. First Corinthians 15:33 (NIV) says, "Do not be misled: 'Bad company corrupts good character.'" Personally, I have no desire to be near a rattlesnake. I certainly do not want to be close enough to touch one. Separate yourself from those who may cause separation between you and pleasing God.

Finally, have you been snake bitten? At this point in David's life, he had experienced a few snakebites – people had injured him severely by their actions. David wanted no more of it, and rightly so. He prayed in verses 1-4 for God to deliver, preserve, and keep him from such attacks. Verbal abuse, in some ways, can be as painful as physical abuse.

My brother who had the rattlesnake had a friend who was bitten by a rattlesnake. It took four vials of antivenin to save him, and he nearly lost his arm. Rattlesnake poison is very powerful, but the antivenin is more powerful. Jesus provided all the antivenin we need when He conquered death, hell, and the grave. If you are suffering from the wound of another, turn to Him Who alone can heal and restore the wounded.

NOTES:

PSALM 141
NEW KING JAMES VERSION

¹ LORD, I cry out to You;
Make haste to me!
Give ear to my voice when I cry out to You.
² Let my prayer be set before You as incense,
The lifting up of my hands as the evening sacrifice.

³ Set a guard, O LORD, over my mouth;
Keep watch over the door of my lips.
⁴ Do not incline my heart to any evil thing,
To practice wicked works
With men who work iniquity;
And do not let me eat of their delicacies.

⁵ Let the righteous strike me;
It shall be a kindness.
And let him rebuke me;
It shall be as excellent oil;
Let my head not refuse it.

For still my prayer is against the deeds of the wicked.
⁶ Their judges are overthrown by the sides of the cliff,
And they hear my words, for they are sweet.
⁷ Our bones are scattered at the mouth of the grave,
As when one plows and breaks up the earth.

⁸ But my eyes are upon You, O GOD the Lord;
In You I take refuge;
Do not leave my soul destitute.
⁹ Keep me from the snares they have laid for me,
And from the traps of the workers of iniquity.
¹⁰ Let the wicked fall into their own nets,
While I escape safely.

71

IVORY SOAP
PSALM 141

Watch your mouth! Somewhere, sometime, someone probably has said something like that to you. I remember one time my mother literally washed my mouth out with soap. If that ever happens to you, ask for anything but Ivory soap. The best I recall, that is what I got and it tasted terrible. However, soap may not leave as bad of a taste as an ill-placed word. I think that was the point my mother was making with the Ivory soap. Her point stood out very clearly, because I remember it over forty years later.

As an adult, I've carelessly said things that I quickly realized I shouldn't have said. The trouble with words is that they cannot be taken back. Many times, I wish I had "do-overs." Maybe I need to remember Ivory soap a little more often.

The psalmist David must have had the same challenge. He prayed, "Set a guard, O Lord, over my mouth; Keep watch over the door of my lips." In our modern vernacular, David could have said it this way: "I may have trouble from time to time controlling my trap, so please help me. I don't want to eat my words!" Notice David talked about the door over his lips. There are times when we need to keep the door to our lips shut! One of the hardest things in the world to do is to control the impulse to speak when we shouldn't. Ephesians 5:3, 4 commands us to not participate in "foolish talking, nor coarse jesting."

I can think of many circumstances in my own life when it would have been better to say nothing. A lot of the strife in this world is the result of ill-timed, misplaced words. Words are among the most powerful forces in the world. It is easy for disagreements to escalate to a war of words. In war, each side keeps increasing its firepower in hopes of subduing the other side. The goal is to win. The problem is that in the war of words, nobody wins.

Jesus taught us in Matthew 5:9, "Blessed are the peacemakers." Notice He didn't say, "Blessed are the troublemakers." With words we can make trouble. Without words (silence) we can make peace. I encourage you to be a peacemaker.

The next time someone says something that irritates you and you want to sharply reply, do your best to withhold comment. If you can hold back words for five minutes, you may be surprised how quickly your desire to fire back will subside. Try it. Five minutes later, the argument may not even matter.

Like me, your nature is to verbally fire back when tempted. We need God's help to guard our mouths. Thankfully, He helps us to grow in the fruit of the Spirit, among which is the fruit of self-control (Galatians 5:22, 23). Fruit is evidence of an object's nature and source. For example, an apple is evidence of an apple tree. The fruit of the Spirit (self-control) is evidence of the indwelling presence of the Holy Spirit. Today, ask God to "set a watch over your lips" so that the fruit of your mouth is evidence of the Holy Spirit within you.

NOTES:

PSALM 142
NEW KING JAMES VERSION

1 I cry out to the LORD with my voice;
With my voice to the LORD I make my supplication.
2 I pour out my complaint before Him;
I declare before Him my trouble.

3 When my spirit was overwhelmed within me,
Then You knew my path.
In the way in which I walk
They have secretly set a snare for me.
4 Look on my right hand and see,
For there is no one who acknowledges me;
Refuge has failed me;
No one cares for my soul.

5 I cried out to You, O LORD:
I said, "You are my refuge,
My portion in the land of the living.
6 Attend to my cry,
For I am brought very low;
Deliver me from my persecutors,
For they are stronger than I.
7 Bring my soul out of prison,
That I may praise Your name;
The righteous shall surround me,
For You shall deal bountifully with me."

72

CAVE VISITORS
PSALM 142

When David wrote Psalm 142, he was hiding from Saul in the Cave of Adullam. A cave can either be a place of refuge or a place of entrapment. If Saul's men had found David trapped in that cave, his life would have been over.

God knows our circumstance and how we feel about it. If you take a moment to read 1 Samuel 22:1, 2 you will see that God sent David encouragement in his distress. God knows just when to send help. His timing is perfect even though we may not understand it. David appeared to be almost at breaking point. In Psalm 142:3 he said, "When my spirit was overwhelmed within me, Then you knew my path." Not only did God know where David was, but He also sent people to encourage him in this secret place. First Samuel 22:1 says as David was hiding in the cave "his brothers and all his father's house heard it, and they went down there to him."

At this point, David had been on the run for some time. His family heard where he was and came to see him. I imagine they were a welcome sight, especially since they probably brought him some good stuff to eat. The next verse also says about 400 men came to David to show their support. These cave visitors were the beginning of David's army.

If you look hard enough, you will see that God is working on your behalf just as He did for David. Although you may not see it at times, God has an army around you. Take time to acknowledge the faithful friends in your life. God even tells us in His Word that His angels are "ministering spirits sent forth to minister for those who will inherit salvation" (Hebrews 1:14). There is a host of heaven to minister on your behalf!

So what do we do when we're in a cave? David didn't just sit in his cave, idly passing the time. Although his emotions were frayed and fear was trying to overtake him, he did not cease being who he was. Just because you're in a cave doesn't mean you are to cave in emotionally! Because David was a worshipper, he cried out to God. He had cave visitors long before his family and friends came. God and His host of angels were with David all the time. He was never alone in that cave, and neither are you.

NOTES:

PSALM 143
NEW KING JAMES VERSION

¹ Hear my prayer, O LORD,
Give ear to my supplications!
In Your faithfulness answer me,
And in Your righteousness.
² Do not enter into judgment with Your servant,
For in Your sight no one living is righteous.

³ For the enemy has persecuted my soul;
He has crushed my life to the ground;
He has made me dwell in darkness,
Like those who have long been dead.
⁴ Therefore my spirit is overwhelmed within me;
My heart within me is distressed.

⁵ I remember the days of old;
I meditate on all Your works;
I muse on the work of Your hands.
⁶ I spread out my hands to You;
My soul longs for You like a thirsty land. Selah

⁷ Answer me speedily, O LORD;
My spirit fails!
Do not hide Your face from me,
Lest I be like those who go down into the pit.
⁸ Cause me to hear Your lovingkindness in the morning,
For in You do I trust;
Cause me to know the way in which I should walk,
For I lift up my soul to You.

⁹ Deliver me, O LORD, from my enemies;
In You I take shelter.
¹⁰ Teach me to do Your will,
For You are my God;
Your Spirit is good.
Lead me in the land of uprightness.

[11] *Revive me, O LORD, for Your name's sake!*
For Your righteousness' sake bring my soul out of trouble.
[12] *In Your mercy cut off my enemies,*
And destroy all those who afflict my soul;
For I am Your servant.

73
GREAT TEACHERS
PSALM 143

I well remember many teachers from my school years. There was Mrs. Metcalf, first grade. Mrs. Romine taught me in the sixth grade. Mr. Morrison taught eighth grade English. I cannot remember a lot of what he taught because I was so enamored with the cool Corvette he drove. I was blessed with some great teachers, but none of them were able to teach me the most important thing in life.

When David asked someone to teach him the most important thing in life, he looked to God. In Psalm 143:10 he said, "Teach me to do Your will, For You are my God." Doing God's will is the most important thing in life. Man cannot teach you God's will for your life because it is individually tailored for each person. His plan for your life is different than His plan for my life. Since God's plan is unique for each of us, we should pray as did David: "Teach me to do Your will."

Following the plan of God is a journey and requires sensitivity to the Lord's direction. Where you are today may not be His will for you ten years from now. Pam and I have chosen to live our lives with our main goal being to do the will of God. We've had moments when following the will of God wasn't easy at first. When God told us to move to Ukraine, I was greatly concerned about moving our young children there. I will never forget the day the Lord said to me as I prayed about my concerns, "My will for you is My will for them." His words liberated me. Since our children were under our care, God would never tell me to do anything harmful to them.

We moved to Ukraine confident it was God's will for all four of us. It wasn't God's will for two parents to drag their children to the mission field. Moving to Ukraine was a wonderful experience for all of us, because it was the will of God for all four of us. Years later, our children say it was one of the best things that our family ever did. The plan of God is always the best for our lives. Of course, there will be challenging moments, but there will always be grace to overcome. For my family, we were in the will of God and are still in the will of God today.

As the hour of the Cross was approaching, Jesus prayed this prayer in the Garden of Gethsemane: "Abba, Father, all things are possible for You. Take this cup away from Me; nevertheless, not what I will, but what You will." For two thousand years, mankind has enjoyed the free gift of salvation through the Lord Jesus Christ for one reason – He was willing to do the will of God. Knowing and doing the will of God for our lives is the most important thing in the world.

As a parent, I can best express my will to my children. With God, it is no different. He alone can best express His will for you to you. Don't look to man for God's plan for your life – only God knows the plan He specifically designed for you! David evidently knew the importance of doing the will of God. I dare you to pray as David did: "Teach me to do Your will, for You are my God; Your Spirit is good. Lead me in the land of uprightness."

PSALM 144
NEW KING JAMES VERSION

¹ *Blessed be the LORD my Rock,*
Who trains my hands for war,
And my fingers for battle—
² *My lovingkindness and my fortress,*
My high tower and my deliverer,
My shield and the One in whom I take refuge,
Who subdues my people under me.

³ *LORD, what is man, that You take knowledge of him?*
Or the son of man, that You are mindful of him?
⁴ *Man is like a breath;*
His days are like a passing shadow.

⁵ *Bow down Your heavens, O LORD, and come down;*
Touch the mountains, and they shall smoke.
⁶ *Flash forth lightning and scatter them;*
Shoot out Your arrows and destroy them.
⁷ *Stretch out Your hand from above;*
Rescue me and deliver me out of great waters,
From the hand of foreigners,
⁸ *Whose mouth speaks lying words,*
And whose right hand is a right hand of falsehood.

⁹ *I will sing a new song to You, O God;*
On a harp of ten strings I will sing praises to You,
¹⁰ *The One who gives salvation to kings,*
Who delivers David His servant from the deadly sword.

¹¹ *Rescue me and deliver me from the hand of foreigners,*
Whose mouth speaks lying words,
And whose right hand is a right hand of falsehood—
¹² *That our sons may be as plants grown up in their youth;*
That our daughters may be as pillars, sculptured in palace style;

¹³ That our barns may be full,
Supplying all kinds of produce;
That our sheep may bring forth thousands
And ten thousands in our fields;
¹⁴ That our oxen may be well laden;
That there be no breaking in or going out;
That there be no outcry in our streets.
¹⁵ Happy are the people who are in such a state;
Happy are the people whose God is the LORD!

74
GREAT KIDS
PSALM 144

Of all things that bring me joy, there is not much that ranks above my children. In fact, I can only think of two things – Jesus and my wife, Pam. Recently, I've learned I'm going to be a grandpa. I can't wait to see where that ranks on the scale! Pam and I are blessed with two great children, Drew and Natalie, who serve God. Psalm 127:3 says, "Children are a heritage from the Lord." I agree. I love them more than they could ever know. An old Chinese proverb says, "To understand the love of a father, you must be a father."

Psalm 144 is a song unto the Lord Who preserves and prospers His people. I believe sometimes the words "prosper" and "prosperity" are greatly misused and misunderstood. In Psalm 144:12-15, David listed the outcome of prosperity. He mentioned full barns, thousands of sheep, and strong oxen, all of which would be a sign of material success in David's day. Certainly, we all rejoice when God affords us those blessings.

However, what did David mention first when talking about prosperity? Children! Verse 12 says, "That our sons may be as plants grown up in their youth; That our daughters may be as pillars, Sculptured in palace style." All of the sheep, oxen, and produce-filled barns in the world are not as important as our children. Please take time today (and every day) to pray over your children. Do it now. You won't be sorry.

As you know, this book is a devotional book. *Devotion* is defined as "profound dedication; consecration." What are you profoundly dedicated to? The verb *devote* is defined as "to concentrate on a particular pursuit, occupation, purpose, or cause." What are you concentrating on pursuing?

Today, begin examining your priorities with your children in light of this psalm. Never let pursuit of career or other interests squeeze out the time you need to invest in your children. Take time today to read Scripture and pray with them.

I had a godly great-aunt who died at the age of 105. She had two sons. One was a minister, while the other did not serve God. Although both these men had the same opportunities, they made different choices. My aunt prayed daily for her wayward son, never losing faith that he would serve the Lord. About two years after her death, her son accepted Christ. He was past 80 years of age himself, and is in heaven with her today.

The dictionary defines prosper as "to be successful or fortunate." My aunt prospered. She was "successful." God does desire to bless His people with the material things we need. However, in my opinion, the highest form of prosperity has nothing to do with material things. Jesus said in Luke 9:25, "For what profit is it to a man if he gains the whole world, and is himself destroyed or lost?" Prosperity in its fullest is to be fortunate enough to have a personal relationship with a loving God. Please never lose sight of what is most important.

Perhaps some of you reading this book have children who are not serving Christ. I encourage you to grab hold of this promise in Isaiah 54:13: "All your children shall be taught by the Lord, And great shall be the peace of your children." As you receive this promise by faith, you will see a change in your children. God's Word is always true!

Psalm 145
New King James Version

¹ I will extol You, my God, O King;
And I will bless Your name forever and ever.
² Every day I will bless You,
And I will praise Your name forever and ever.
³ Great is the LORD, and greatly to be praised;
And His greatness is unsearchable.

⁴ One generation shall praise Your works to another,
And shall declare Your mighty acts.
⁵ I will meditate on the glorious splendor of Your majesty,
And on Your wondrous works.
⁶ Men shall speak of the might of Your awesome acts,
And I will declare Your greatness.
⁷ They shall utter the memory of Your great goodness,
And shall sing of Your righteousness.

⁸ The LORD is gracious and full of compassion,
Slow to anger and great in mercy.
⁹ The LORD is good to all,
And His tender mercies are over all His works.

¹⁰ All Your works shall praise You, O LORD,
And Your saints shall bless You.
¹¹ They shall speak of the glory of Your kingdom,
And talk of Your power,
¹² To make known to the sons of men His mighty acts,
And the glorious majesty of His kingdom.
¹³ Your kingdom is an everlasting kingdom,
And Your dominion endures throughout all generations.

¹⁴ The LORD upholds all who fall,
And raises up all who are bowed down.
¹⁵ The eyes of all look expectantly to You,
And You give them their food in due season.
¹⁶ You open Your hand
And satisfy the desire of every living thing.

*¹⁷ The LORD is righteous in all His ways,
Gracious in all His works.
¹⁸ The LORD is near to all who call upon Him,
To all who call upon Him in truth.
¹⁹ He will fulfill the desire of those who fear Him;
He also will hear their cry and save them.
²⁰ The LORD preserves all who love Him,
But all the wicked He will destroy.
²¹ My mouth shall speak the praise of the LORD,
And all flesh shall bless His holy name
Forever and ever.*

75

GRAVY OVER ALL
PSALM 145

In my hometown there is a famous restaurant named Murphy's Steakhouse. Their signature dish is called a Hot Hamburger, which consists of two pieces of toast covered by a large hamburger patty piled high with fresh-cut French fries. An optional side dish is a special recipe of gravy, which can be poured over the entire plate. When you order, if you desire the gravy on the hot hamburger, you say "gravy over all." The now deceased founder made those words famous and has those words inscribed on his tombstone.

The word "all" appears in Psalm 145 at least fourteen times. "All" is the most inclusive word in the English language. It covers everything, just like the gravy. When the gravy is poured, because it is liquid, it runs over all the fried potatoes, meat patty, and toast. There is nothing on the plate untouched by the gravy. Let's consider some of the "alls" in this psalm.

- Psalm 145:9—"The Lord is good to all."
- Psalm 145:13—"Your dominion endures throughout all generations."
- Psalm 145:14—"The Lord upholds all who fall, And raises up all who are bowed down."
- Psalm 145:17—"The Lord is righteous in all His ways, gracious in all His works."
- Psalm 145:18—"The Lord is near to all who call upon Him."

- Psalm 145:20—"The Lord preserves all who love Him."

If there is anything I would like for you to remember from this book, it is that God has everything covered for you. You will never face a circumstance for which He does not have an answer. You will never commit an act that He will not forgive if you repent. He forgives all.

Let's go back to the gravy metaphor. Take a moment to picture your life as the big plate of hot hamburger with every French fry symbolizing a segment or event in your life. When that gravy is poured over it, everything is touched and covered. Jesus covers all our sins, all our faults, all of our failures. He heals all our diseases (Psalm 103:3). He has you covered.

In war movies, a brave soldier charges toward an enemy position as another soldier says, "I've got you covered." While the first soldier advances to his position, the second is firing away at the enemy, making sure he is safe. As you proceed through the battleground of life, God has you covered. Through Christ He has provided everything you will ever need. I leave you with this encouragement from Psalm 103:2: "Forget not all His benefits." They are more than enough!

REFERENCES

Dake, Finis Jennings. Dake's Annotated Reference Bible. Dake Bible Sales, Lawrenceville, GA, 1963.

Sander, Stanley. The Korean War: An Encyclopedia. 1995.

Spirit Filled Life Bible. Thomas Nelson Inc., Nashville, TN, 1991.

The New Open Bible, Study Edition, The New King James Version. Thomas Nelson Inc., Nashville, TN, 1990.

Zuck, Roy B.; Walvoord, John F. The Bible Knowledge Commentary. Dallas Theological Seminary, Victor / Cook Communications, Dallas, TX.

www.allaboutphilosophy.org/life-of-king-david.htm. Accessed August 2009.

Acknowledgements

I want to express deep gratitude to Mica Kilstrom for her excellent editorial help. Matt Jones, you did a great job with the artwork and typesetting. You both have a very bright future.

Karen Hardin, I thank you for your professional advice on writing, editing, and publishing. You always steered me the right direction. Neil Kingsley at Press Group, you were always available and you have been a delight to work with.

To my fabulous wife, Pam, you are amazing and this book would have been impossible without you. I should warn you there are two more in the works. We have never lived in a cave, but you have followed me to some wild places. Thank you for pushing me forward.

Most of all, I must say to my Heavenly Father, thank You for putting it in my heart to write and then telling me to do it. Forgive me for being slow to respond. I am going to keep writing.

BIOGRAPHY

Jim King, and his wife Pam, have been in full-time ministry since 1976. In addition to their calling of evangelism, they have been active in overseas evangelism, church planting and development, humanitarian relief, and orphanages.

Since 1992, the ministry has established over 280 DVD formatted Bible schools, and sponsored over 180 new churches in Eastern Europe and the Middle East. The most recent church plants have been in Israel.

In 1995, the Kings established a humanitarian fund focused on answering the cries of the less fortunate. One result has been establishing House of Joy orphanage in Kahovka, Ukraine.

The ministry the Lord has entrusted to the Kings has taken them to places such as Brazil, Cuba, Russia, Siberia, Ukraine, South Korea, China, Israel, Romania, India, North Korea, Turkey and many others.

Jim and Pam have hosted scores of teams on overseas missions trips and Holy Land tours. The ministry maintains offices in Kiev and Kahovka, Ukraine and Tulsa, OK. Jim and Pam have two married children, son, Drew and Jenny King, and daughter, Natalie and Eric Morris.

In addition to their overseas ministry, Jim and Pam are actively committed to an extensive speaking schedule in churches and conferences across the nation. You may contact the Kings at:

Jim King Ministries
P. O. Box 700221
Tulsa, OK 74170-0221

918-494-7772
info@jimking.org
www.jimking.org